"The social, political, and economic problems of our critical period cannot be understood or solved unless we understand social, political, and economic trends. Trends suggest change, evolution, both in man's way of thinking and in man's environment. Upon the natural environment man has imposed an artificial one of his own. That artificial environment has had profound effects upon him—changed his community life, given him powers far beyond those with which he is naturally endowed. The trend of society, then, reveals a process of social adaptation to the artificial environment.

"How is this evolution, this trend, to be presented in simple terms that any intelligent reader can grasp? Dr. Otto Neurath has addressed himself to this task with a success which could have been achieved only by a man of his long experience and fine imagination. As the former director of the Museum of Social Sciences of Vienna and the creator of the now widely introduced 'Viennese method' of elucidating facts pictorially he knew precisely what facts should be presented and above all how they should be presented.

"*Dr. Neurath has given us what is to my mind a remarkable, a unique book.* His ingeniously conceived and skillfully executed pictures are not merely illustrations but integral parts of the text. Moreover each picture is confined to the explanation of a single fact or a single set of social circumstances. It can be grasped at a glance. So with the text. No words are wasted. Academic terminology is usually avoided, and where it is unavoidable it is explained.

"As a consequence of this treatment Dr. Neurath's book has a dynamic

The Survey Graphic the imagination on fire as Van Loon, or H. G. Wells, sometimes does simply by giving us a surprising glimpse of ourselves in a moving social procession . . . Back of Neurath's pictures lie profound research, statistics transformed into ideas, ideas then designed into a picture narrative, a drama of social interpretation. . . . Few men of our time have laid their hands so close to the dramatic plot that marks our destiny on this planet."

Modern Man in the Making

Modern Man in the Making

Otto Neurath

Director, International Foundation for Visual Education

Alfred • A • Knopf • New York & London • 1939

Foreword

An ordinary reporter deals with persons whom he has met or with events which he has himself experienced, whereas this book deals with social facts of world-wide import. Nations, classes, states, well-to-do and poor people are described by means of simple charts and simple statements in this report, without the use of personal names. An attempt has been made to evolve for this purpose a special picture-text style which should enable anybody to walk through the modern world that is beginning to appear about us and see it as he may see a landscape with its hills and plains, woods and meadows.

The aim is to trace the origin of "modern men" and depict their behaviour and achievements, without presenting any social or economic theory. No attempt has been made to define the term "modern." It appears from the ordinary use of the word that an institution or a custom may be called "modern" if there is any scientific reason to assume that it displays a certain social trend and if it is being imitated to a world-wide extent.

This comprehensive survey starts with facts. The same fact can be looked at from different points of view. Thus it may be an element in the world situation, or an element in the total social environment, or an element of daily life. It is important to build bridges from one field of investigation to another and to show cross-connexions.

Modernity as a universal phenomenon is widely discussed. Certain arguments appear again and again, but are scattered so that it is not easy to arrive at a comprehensive view. How can facts be presented without causing confusion by their overwhelming diversity? The visualization of selected primary material connected with simple statements is one solution.

Even such "selection" influences readers in a certain direction, but one can interpret the same facts in different senses and augment them. That is one important difference between a merely general argument and an explanation based on a collection of facts. It is not everybody's business to read bulky scientific books and to analyse statistical data, which combine information from different sources. Therefore this book presents, where possible, material which everybody will find useful in interpreting statistics published in newspapers or reference books.

The principle of visualization applied in this book is based on the ISOTYPE method, developed by me together with my collaborators during the last fifteen years. It shows connexions between facts instead of discussing them. Impressive visual aids do not merely act as illustrations or as eye-bait in this book; they are parts of the explanations themselves. The reader may not understand the contents by reading the text only; he must "read" the pictures as carefully as the text. An international picture language is combined with a word language.

It is not easy to describe universal social facts. International data concerning the present and suitable for comparison are not readily found, and very few concerning the past are available; hence one must deal with such figures as are at one's disposal. Birth and death appear more frequently in this book than their social importance warrants, because more data dealing with birth and death are available than of any other kind. These data must therefore be used as interpretative aids.

Everybody, even one who is no scholar, is able to take a scientific attitude and to regard calmly the Pilgrimage of Man—the life, fears, and hopes of large groups of people rather than of single persons. Heroes, kings, leaders, scientists, actors, or other individuals are interesting subjects of investigation and description, but must be treated differently from mankind as a whole.

Fear and hope worry men. Walt Whitman's "There was never any more inception than there is now . . . and will never be any more perfection than there is now, nor any more heaven or hell than there is now," may perhaps be a consolation for many people in difficult social situations. Nevertheless not a few want to know what inception, what perfection, what particular kind of heaven or hell ours may be. Goethe's saying that "a philistine is an empty sausage-skin, stuffed with fear and hope," characterizes not only a certain group of people, but all; it is impossible to be sure of finding exceptions. The scientific attitude seems to reduce uneasiness and disturbance a little by analysing a situation. Science has been an important tool for mankind and may continue to be so in the future.

The combination of the desire for security with the desire for adventure is inherently human, but the desire for security may lead to social organization, which the desire for adventure does not. Where does fresh security and where does fresh insecurity arise? That is the question. Philosophers, theologians, poets, politicians, journalists, pedagogues, scientists, and men in the street are trying to answer this question. By modern means, as a human being of our time, I shall try to tell about our environment, about you and about myself; but in a general way. So, but without Walt Whitman's unceasing enthusiasm, "the Modern Man I sing."

Contents

pression. Mankind and preparation for war. Restricted production and destroyed products. "Autarchy" as a destroyer and teacher. Relief work and the armament industry as brothers. Best sellers tell about war, commerce, and piracy. War economy. Necessity makes strange bedfellows. Planning and civil liberty. War is more easily planned than peace. Is war necessary? How to engineer a real world community.

Profile of happiness. From the first-class travellers to the hoboes. Modern men have a thick skin. The ruling groups in commerce and government. Social discrimination, old and new. To what extent do strikes express the degree of discontent? Elections and publicity. Chessboard of three politico-economic qualities. Who may become whose ally? Co-operation in fighting floods and establishing irrigation. Those who fear centralization. Stocks of goods and the prevention of famine. Does increase of facilities for communication also mean an increase of freedom of speech? The territory of modernity.

Child without uncle. Why are there kindergartens? Women's "veils" are vanishing. Leisure is victorious. Sports and militarism. Uniforms and flirtation. Increase of recreation and education in modern life. The age of refrigerators, bathtubs, and electric bulbs. From noon meal to dinner. Fun and pleasure. Rhythm of personal life. The extent of the traveller's world. Features of death. Traditional rules and premarital sex relations. Love and business. "The boss will fire me." What is the result of social instability? Magical traditions and the scientific attitude. What has become of the thirteenth floor? The change in man's character and man's social order. Reconstruction of social order and the life of modern man.

Bibliography and quotations.

Past and Present

Can one visualize, in a single picture, basic changes in the life mode of modern man—that is, in elements which change not only his technical equipment, but also his hopes and fears? Of course one can. Modern people live longer than their forefathers did. Therefore improvement in public health is a characteristic feature of modern history.

Mortality Rates in a Central European Town

Sixteenth and seventeenth centuries

1591 ✝✝✝

1599 Plague ✝✝✝✝✝✝✝✝✝✝ ✝✝✝✝✝✝✝✝✝✝

1624 ✝✝✝✝

1626 Plague ✝✝✝✝✝✝✝✝✝✝ ✝✝✝✝✝✝✝✝✝✝ ✝✝✝✝✝✝✝✝✝✝

1656 ✝✝✝✝✝

1657 Plague ✝✝✝✝✝✝✝✝✝✝ ✝✝✝✝✝✝✝✝✝✝ ✝✝✝✝✝✝✝✝

1663 ✝✝✝✝

Eighteenth, nineteenth and twentieth centuries

1783 ✝✝✝

1830 ✝✝✝

1880 ✝✝✝

1900 ✝✝

1913 ✝✝

1918 War ✝✝✝

1936 ✝✝

Each cross represents 1 death per 100 population

13

Unemployment Cycles

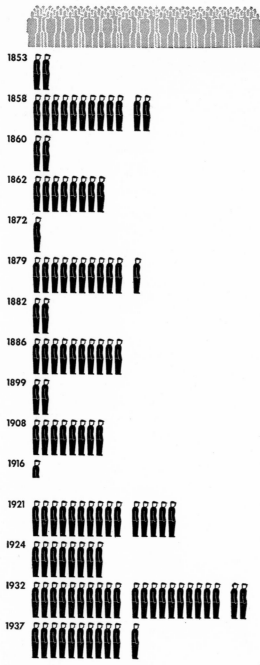

Each symbol represents
1 % unemployed among members of British Trade Unions

14

Realize what multifarious changes in human life followed the release of Europeans from the plague. The Black Death in the fourteenth century destroyed families and human contacts, customs, and traditions. A third of Europe's and perhaps of the world's population died. The plague struck rich and poor—kings and popes, painters and scientists, as well as the man in the street. Bit by bit authorities combated the plague by quarantine and other measures.

Is this an example of the complete elimination of fluctuations in security?

Not at all! A tremendous rise and fall in fear and trouble is apparent, corresponding with the increase and decrease of unemployment in Western countries, similar to the rise and fall in death-rates. These new fluctuations, combined with pauperism, began to strike men after the invasions of the plague ended.

People learned to fight epidemics centuries ago. A tendency to fight unemployment and its causes is becoming more evident. Unemployment and pauperism do not menace everyone as directly as the plague did. If poverty were infectious, it might have disappeared like the plague. But economic depressions threaten larger groups of people than formerly. The fear of economic depressions, wars, revolutions, and counter-revolutions takes the place of fear of the plague. To remove these growing dangers would involve serious alterations of some major social institutions. The fight against the plague was possible without any important social changes.

The plague came from the unknown, spread everywhere, and vanished, nobody knew why. There was a common fear of this terrifying unknown.

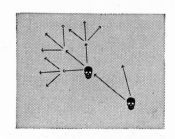

Local barriers were erected, but they were not very efficient. State and town officials shrank from calling the disease by its name, fearing that commercial interests would suffer.

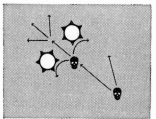

The growing power of governments made a more efficient organization possible. Extended cordons of police kept the plague outside western and central Europe.

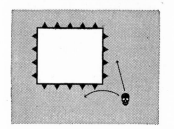

The international health organization of the League of Nations restricts the plague to a relatively small territory in Asia. The protected region is now almost the whole world.

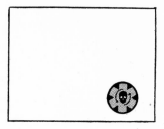

Fighting menaces coming from geographically unknown sources continued for centuries. The nomad was the bearer of another menace. Nomadic tribes and nations—the Huns and later the Arabs, the Mongols, and the Turks—terrified European countries, up to the times when the Europeans themselves began to become the "scourges" of the natives in Africa, Asia, America, and Australia. One cannot easily reconstruct the horror which was spread by the invading masses of Huns and Mongols. Today one knows that there are no longer unknown masses in motion to surprise men by a sudden attack. Our knowledge of the world is becoming so clear that even those forces which menaced our ancestors have been traced to their sources.

They came from the steppes in central Asia.

Nomadic Invasions from Central Asia   red lines: routes of nomads

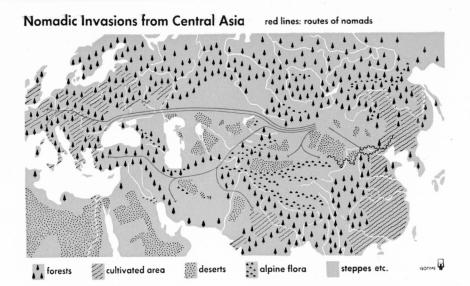

▲ forests   /// cultivated area   ⣿ deserts   ⣿ alpine flora   ▬ steppes etc.   ISOTYPE

Scarcity of food kept the people in central Asia constantly on the move. To-day it is known that, for instance, the Lop Nor lake in central Asia changed its position. That meant the disappearance of fertile land, of the livelihood of whole peoples. There may be many other causes which put masses in motion. There were no geographic barriers against warlike migrations. The Chinese erected their famous wall and defended their Empire against invasions. The expansion of the Russian Empire ended the pressure of Asiatic nomads against Europe. Russian settlers went to the East along the rivers of Siberia, following the custom of the old Northmen who carried their boats from river to river. The mystic forces of the East vanished: Gog and Magog, the Biblical kings, and their followers.

Outer Mongolia

Outer Mongolia and Tannu Tuva, depending upon their great neighbours, are the heirs of an old tradition. They are, as it were, the remnant of the former unknown.

16

Modern scientific methods and engineering have spread over the whole world, especially the technology of war, which is the backbone of the political and social life of the present time. The elimination of the strange is necessarily accompanied by unification. Photographs of a League of Nations Congress or of an international naval conference reveal Western dress and Western uniform with very few exceptions. Progress from the colourful multifarious picture of the arms and weapons of the past up to the egalitarian sameness of modern uniforms is symbolic:

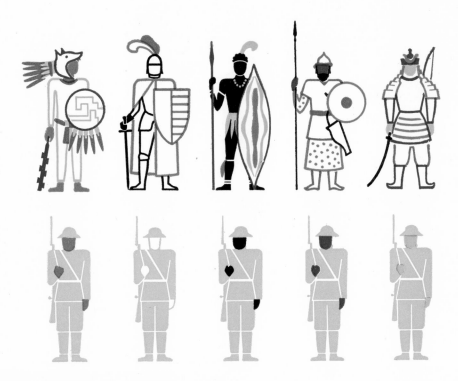

As a matter of fact, this unification is far advanced. In the international market, industries which use cheap labour and relatively primitive machinery can compete successfully with highly developed industries. On the battlefield victories are won by the most highly developed war equipment. Whatever the social order may be, a knowledge of war technology is the common possession of all nations today. Cheap armament and badly fed soldiers do not win battles. Mankind disposes of better equipment, better planning, and better methods for killing and tormenting fellow-beings than for making life and living-conditions secure.

Is there any evidence of increasing security? Can mankind be shielded from the unknown? Certainly not. There is in the world much fear of the unpredictable. Belief in an increasing general security has been shaken by the events of the last decades. Nowadays people fear one another more than they fear unknown forces.

Still, there are many examples in history of arms which had been made for war eventually being used constructively for peace. Will international co-operation in the future apply technology solely to achieve human happiness?

Unification of Mankind

From time immemorial tribes and peoples influenced one another successively. Customs and words, tales and tools wandered throughout the world and linked African with Eurasian peoples, the latter with arctic tribes, and islanders of the Pacific with Americans. It is hardly possible to say which people were the first to use the plough or which first tamed the horse to become a helper of man. All these innovations spread.

Probably the first civilizations owed their existence to a common struggle against natural forces, such as floods and droughts. The first states organized the struggle. The Mediterranean civilizations were developed more or less in isolation, as in the valley of the Nile, of the Euphrates and Tigris, and in southern Arabia. Such civilizations may easily be destroyed. Ruins of old Arabian towns are found abandoned in deserts.

Such isolation is broken down by roads and other connexions. Still, a fairly definite line separates the Old World from the New.

Birthplaces of Civilization

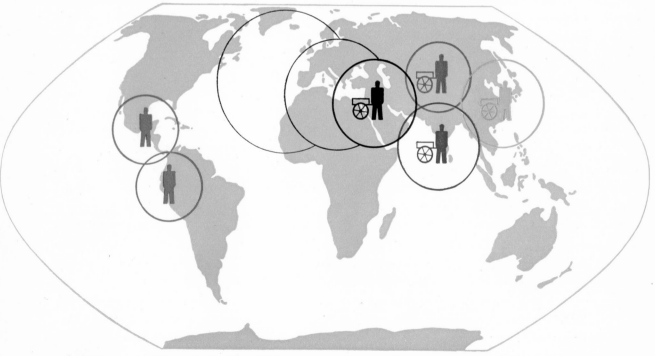

red: old American (without wheel)   black: Mediterranean   brown: Indian   green: Central Asiatic   yellow: Far Eastern

The pre-Columbian civilization of America was highly developed in agriculture, horticulture, astronomy, mathematics, and writing. But it had no wheel nor draught animal, especially no horse. Traces of a very early prehistoric horse have been found in America, which later became extinct. The wheel seems to be a very special invention. There is no part of the human body which suggests the wheel turning round a separate axle, as for instance an extended arm suggests the hammer. We find the wheel in use in all civilizations of the Old World, in various forms. It came to America only with the Spanish conquistadores.

Modern civilization is based mainly on Mediterranean ways and customs; it preserves in particular the traditions and experience of mediæval Roman Catholic and Greek Orthodox peoples and of the ancient Roman Empire. Modern world society is the successor of mediæval and ancient Roman society. The Roman Empire comprehended all the peoples who lived around the Mediterranean. Hence Christian names are of Latin, Greek, Jewish, Teutonic, and Anglo-Saxon, but not of Arabian, Indian, or Chinese origin. From Latin: Anthony, Austin, Cecil, Felix, Julius, Patrick, Vincent, Clara, Gloria, Grace, June, Lucy; from Greek: Alexander, Andrew, Eugene, George, Isidore, Peter, Philip, Barbara, Catherine, Dorothy, Helen, Margaret; from Hebrew: Daniel, James, John, Matthew, Michael, Samuel, Thomas, Anna, Elizabeth, Mary, Susan; from Teutonic: Adolph, Arnold, Charles, Louis, Richard, Rudolph, William, Amelia; from Anglo-Saxon: Edgar, Elmer, Edith, Ethel, Hilda.

The influence of Arabic civilization was not so great. It began after A.D. 700. Christian, Jewish, and Arabic philosophy were united during the Middle Ages by a common religious and scientific tradition. Some social, military, and technical activities of European nations were influenced directly by the Arabian world. So, too, were a great many nations in Africa and Asia. Among our everyday words, some are of Arabian origin, such as: admiral, alcohol, arsenal, alkali, apricot, candy, chemicals, coffee, drug, tariff, traffic. If it is true that the Arabian word *al-kimiya* is derived from a Greek word, *chymeia*, meaning "a mingling," the word *alchemy* would still be a symbol of the close connexion between ancient Mediterranean cultures.

Scholars point out that numerous Western doctrines derive from East Indian counterparts, but the social behaviour of Western people was not essentially changed by the notions and activities—or, rather, inactivities—of the Hindus, nor by their caste system or suttee. The Buddhist's shrinking from the horrors of war and slaughter has only a few counterparts in Western history. The real efforts of Indian kings to organize peace for the sake of peace have no equivalents in the history of the Crusades, with their bloodshed, or in that of the Holy Roman Empire.

There is a direct and indirect Chinese influence on modern technology, such as in the use of paper, porcelain, silk, and rockets. We accept as our own fruits that originated in China, such as oranges, peaches, apricots. Likewise the Chinese received many vegetables from Europe.

Europeans who penetrated into China in the fourteenth century were welcomed and accepted as collaborators by the government. After they returned to Europe, they told of a well-organized and well-educated nation. Good relations between representatives of the Catholic Church and the Chinese rulers followed and were maintained for a long time. Because of their superior weapons, Europeans began to look down on the Chinese. Certain Chinese moral and political doctrines stimulated European thinkers and reformers, however, especially in the eighteenth century. During the rococo period the design of Western furniture reflected Chinese influence.

From the very beginning of the industrial revolution which rapidly spread over the world, Christian peoples widely influenced the social behaviour of "infidel" nations in Asia and Africa, such as the Japanese, Chinese, Hindus, Iranians, Turks, Arabs, Moors, and Negroes. On the other hand the general attitude and the conditioned reactions of modern men are not influenced to any remarkable degree by the behaviour of these peoples in our age.

Political organization means much in civilization. The history of the great powers shows how governments extend their influence over the individual, preparing war or organizing internal peace, preventing floods and famines, erecting road and irrigation systems, regulating cities and social institutions.

Nations can work out successfully only what they have learned in past centuries. Modern organization is based on experience within world imperia. Europeans learned self-government in the Middle Ages, established "urban republics," and, if necessary, stopped fighting between small groups—between family and family, between fortified palace and fortified palace within one town, as in Italy—for their ancestors had experienced the internal peace of the Roman Empire. Comprehensive state organization similar to the organization of world imperia ended most such conflicts in modern times. The Mohammedans were forced to suppress the old revenge for blood when they became conquerors; no big army can be based on a cooperation of avengers. Internal peace was sometimes only a period of preparation for war. Arabian caliphs as temporal and spiritual rulers of their nation, no less than Mongolian khans, were setting little stones of the mosaic of "world peace," the day-dream of modern times.

If we apply the name "world imperium" only to such realms as have contained about twenty-five per cent of the world population, we find no more than five imperia from the Roman Empire down to the present time.

World Imperia

A.D.

Imperium Romanum   China

800

Arabian Empire

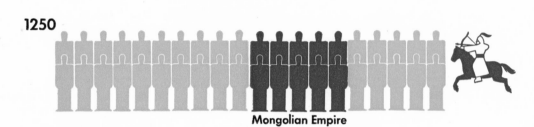

1250

Mongolian Empire

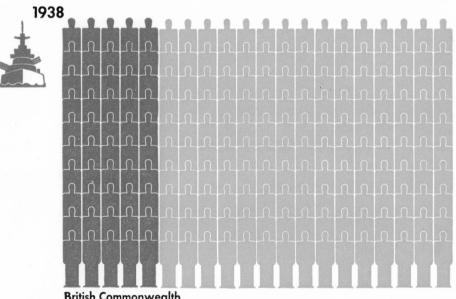

1938

British Commonwealth
of Nations

Each man symbol represents 10 million population

ISOTYPE

24

The Imperium Romanum, the predecessor of the British Commonwealth of Nations, the characteristic world imperium of our times, was of a different structure. Like the Chinese Empire, it may be regarded as a gigantic fortification with walls and towers.

The Roman and Chinese Empires

These empires were brought into contact with each other by trade in Chinese silk and Roman metal, glass, dyestuffs, and drugs.

The Silk Roads between the Ancient Roman and Chinese Empires

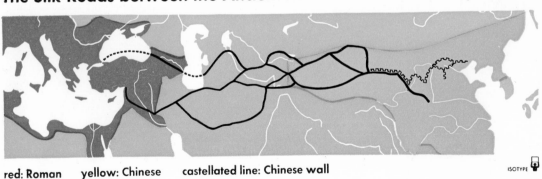

red: Roman   yellow: Chinese   castellated line: Chinese wall

ISOTYPE

25

Their knowledge of each other was rather vague, since this trade was in the hands of some tribes and states in central and western Asia. The fact that a few Romans penetrated into China was of no importance. Overseas trade was in its infancy when the plague, internal disturbances, and diminishing resistance against the invasions of barbarians menaced both empires and all possibility of peaceful intercourse or well-organized war.

The Chinese wall was built to protect the valley of the Yellow River and the road to western dependencies against invasions by the Huns and other nomadic tribes of the steppes in the north-west of China. This road to the west was frequented in the first century after the birth of Christ, the period when the silk trade with the Roman Empire flourished. The direction of the Silk Road changed according to political necessity, and perhaps also according to natural conditions. It intersected the Lop Nor oasis and followed the lake when, as a result of some natural phenomenon, the lake altered its location. Walls protected China from external aggression till the twelfth century.

The Roman walls, erected against disturbing invasions of uncivilized tribes, had to protect a system of towns and a network of connecting roads.

Roman Towns, Roads and Walls

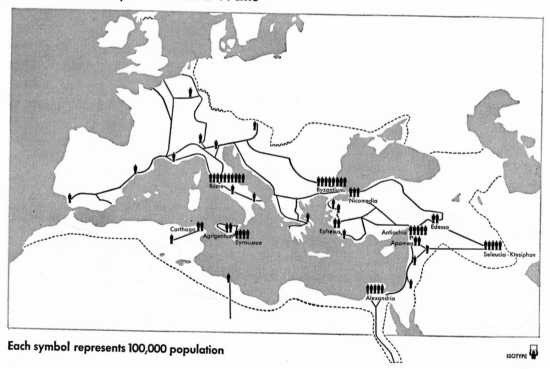

Each symbol represents 100,000 population

The Roman Empire was the prototype of Western government and jurisdiction. Roman law, the direct ancestor of much Western law and a strong influence on all modern law, arose from a specific historical situation. The Roman Empire united the different civilizations of the Mediterranean region, comprising highly developed but also primitive peoples, and occasionally destroyed centres of ancient civilization, such as Carthage, Corinth, and other cities. The nucleus was agrarian, but commercial evolution began very early. Roman peasants were the best warriors of the Mediterranean. They were eager for battle and fought bravely; the armies gained much booty. Conquests often paid the army directly and enriched Roman citizens. Rome became the capital of an enormous realm, but not a centre of manufacturing industry as the Greek and Hellenistic cities did. It was the chief consumer and the money centre. While Greek colonies had mostly been self-governing, Roman colonies depended upon the capital; they were new Roman areas populated by Roman peasants and Roman soldiers. The military roads were well organized and were used for travelling and by the Roman postal system as well as by the Roman legions. This Mediterranean civilization was similar, in certain respects, to that of the last few centuries.

In those ancient times the fact became known that sometimes profits rise as products become scarce. The Egyptians destroyed papyrus when too much of it grew and prices fell.

Bureaucratic centralization became stronger in the eastern part of the Roman Empire. The later Byzantine Empire, which separated from Rome in early Christian times, had a very highly developed state organization, which even evolved a sort of state economy. In many respects modern attempts at planning a national economy can be based on Byzantine tradition more than on Roman. But the term "Byzantinism" seems to indicate something far from modern—an antagonism of West and East.

Both of the following world imperia were founded by nomads. They had much less inner stability. The Arabian Empire, primarily a military organization of nomadic tribes, progressed step by step to urban life, science, technology, libraries, universities, and other institutions which are the predecessors of modern ones. The Arabs were very well organized. They developed new cavalry tactics and thus forced Western countries to change their methods of waging battle.

The Mongols, without close contact with agriculture and urban culture, knowing hardly anything but a pastoral life and war, often regarded towns as heaps of stones that intruded on pasture-land. Along with the towns they destroyed irrigation systems and put an end to the fertility of the Euphrates and Tigris valleys, which are still arid. Expanding in vast but thinly populated regions, their Empire embraced not more than twenty-five per cent of mankind, yet covered the largest area ever united under one government. They had a well-organized system of roads,

The Arabian Empire

The Mongolian Empire

28

which was the basis of the political organization of a colossal empire. After the first steps of conquest and destruction the khans quickly adopted the culture of the subjugated people. The khans in China were the most modern governors of their time, tolerating every religion and seeking the advice of craftsmen, engineers, and scientists of many nations. Perhaps Mongols promoted the art of printing, which spread westward and influenced the Renaissance. The Mongols stopped their victorious invasion of Europe when the Great Khan died (1227).

No European world imperium, according to our crude definition, was erected during the Middle Ages. The British Commonwealth of Nations, the world imperium of the last few centuries, does not command an overwhelming force as the Roman Empire did. It is one of the big units that maintain the balance of world power, like the United States, the Soviet Union, France, Germany, Japan, and Italy. Its fleet is the largest in the world, though no longer so predominant as it was. Every growing naval power is a danger to Britain. Like any other power, the British Empire cannot protect itself without allies.

The British Commonwealth of Nations

The British Commonwealth of Nations is a new type of empire, with its components scattered over the whole earth. The map of the British Commonwealth in itself symbolizes the fact that there are no more unknown territories. The neighbours of the Roman Empire were of a lower type of civilization. The British Empire has neighbours of equal social standing. An insular empire is today impossible. The Romans called their neighbours "barbarians"; the Britons met most of theirs as members of the League of Nations. These neighbours are scattered over the whole world.

What people have thought of by "world unity" has varied. At the time of the first discoveries in Central America pacifistic people spoke of a Christian peace which excluded the Turks. The limitations of peace were narrower than geographical knowledge. About two hundred years later, still only Christian countries were admitted to the family of civilized nations.

The Treaty of Westphalia signed by the German Emperor and the French King, to settle disputes between a number of countries, was thought to be almost "worldwide." This is the region affected:

The Westphalian Treaty, after the Thirty Years' War in Germany, 1648

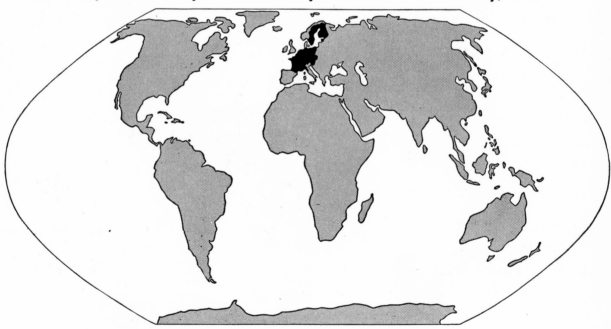

Black: signatory powers and countries concerned

The Christian nations—Turkey excluded—may best be visualized by the area of the countries which were brought together by the Congress of Vienna:

Congress of Vienna, after the Napoleonic Wars, 1814

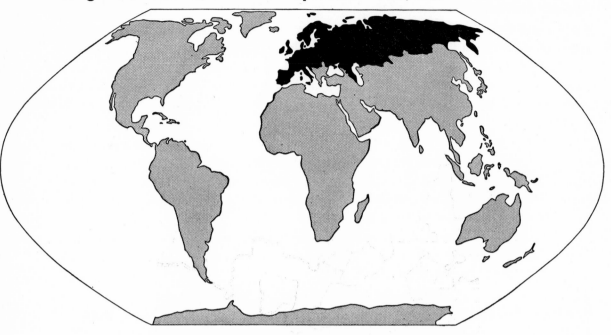

The treaties of Versailles, Saint-Germain and Trianon included even peoples living far from Christian faith, and some of the signers were coloured.

Peace Treaties after the World War

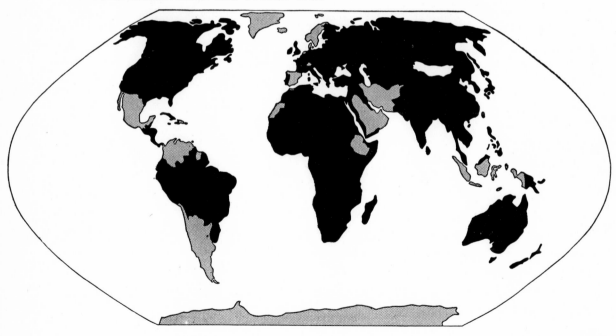

And what of the Hapsburg Empire? It did not contain twenty-five per cent of the world population, and it was not a consistent empire like the others mentioned above. The Holy Roman Empire of the Middle Ages was unlike the ancient Roman Empire. It was a conglomeration of feudalistic regions.

A Part of Germany in the Sixteenth Century

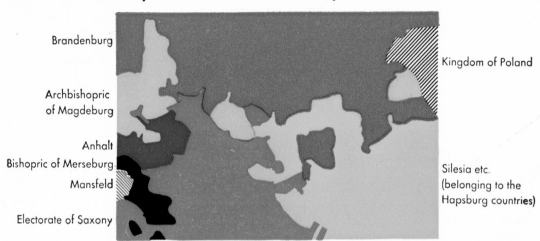

Brandenburg

Archbishopric
of Magdeburg

Anhalt
Bishopric of Merseburg
Mansfeld

Electorate of Saxony

Kingdom of Poland

Silesia etc.
(belonging to the
Hapsburg countries)

The Hapsburg Empire was not based on a central power or a central organization. By marriages, by heritage of titles and different rights, the Hapsburgs brought under their rule the Netherlands and Spain, Hungary, Alsace, and parts of Italy. Before the Hapsburgs came into power in Spain, about 1500, the expulsion of the Moors and Jews had already started, during the fifteenth century, and with them the most highly developed part of the population. Many libraries were destroyed, in the name of the Holy Catholic Church. Courageous adventurers from Spain and Portugal went to Africa and later westward, thus introducing their feudal customs abroad.

Aztec weapons had never been forced to compete with European weapons before the Spanish conquistadores landed on the Mexican coast about A.D. 1500. After the conquest Indian kings and priests, commoners and serfs perished in widespread slaughter, but the decrease in population was a continuation of a decrease which had begun before; war and human sacrifice had decimated the natives. Those who were killed by the conquistadores had themselves been killers and tormentors of their fellow-beings:

Population of Latin America

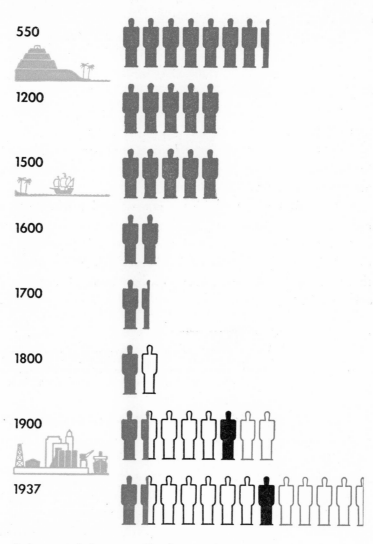

550

1200

1500

1600

1700

1800

1900

1937

Each man symbol represents 10 million population

red, full: Indian   black, outlined: white   black, full: Negro   red, outlined: mixed

ISOTYPE

After that cities with temples, palaces, houses, mud and log huts, monuments and tombs, paintings and manuscripts were destroyed or buried and old traditions were concealed in a new social order. New customs were combined with old ones which continued their existence under some cloak: "This dark Madonna was the heathen goddess Tonantzin before she was the mother of Christ." The Europeans could not always destroy or hide the ancient customs and beliefs.

Later the Spaniards found that the silver and gold they wanted had to be taken from inside mountains; they needed Indian labour. As landlords they also needed Indian labour to cultivate plantations. As adventurers they needed Indian wives and so created a population of mixed blood.

The attitude of the North American colonists, at least in the Northern states, was different. They were settlers with wives and children, and most of them needed Indian soil. In Latin America Indian traditions are beginning to be re-established; in English-speaking North America Indian reservations are maintaining what remains of old tribal communities.

The red Indians could not stand hard work. They died in masses under the pressure of their masters. That is one reason why Negroes were transported into certain American regions, and sometimes priests supported this action in the hope that their poor red brothers would be saved. When commerce and profit developed, this new slavery was exploited in a flourishing trade; the Negroes were packed like sardines in tins:

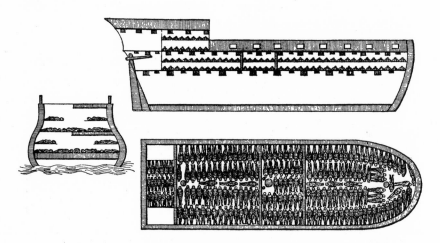

The efficient merchants of that time so organized the traffic in slaves that the loss by deaths did not nullify the advantage of cheap transport. At first slavery helped to expand feudalism on a new basis, always combined with commercial organization. At the same time the old feudal organization of society was disappearing in Europe. In England and other countries of northern Europe the industrial revolution was loosening the patriarchal relation between lords and dependants. Great

34

masses of proletarians were rising. Under changing conditions the colonists of America adopted the Spanish scheme of importing Negro labour, and they continued to do so up to the middle of the nineteenth century, on a larger scale than ever before.

These transplantations of masses of men contributed much to the unification of mankind by adding millions of primitives to the masses of proletarians. This has had an important influence on the present social situation, especially in the United States. Not only the fact that people of African origin are living in America, but also the fact that they were brought there against their will, that they were separated from their families, that they were forced to work for their masters, that they were bought and sold like goods, that they were bred like animals, that they were slaves—not only slaves in the sense of antiquity, slaves by misfortune, but slaves of a so-called low and detestable origin—this could not but deeply impress the unfortunates and end in insurrections. Many humanitarians supported the slaves' claim for freedom, and even governments suggested the abolition of slavery. Sometimes that meant weakening a competitor. When the slaves were really freed, they found themselves on the lowest proletarian level, unable to return to the free, primitive life of their ancestors. No longer dependent on the decision of one man, they were dependent on the general business situation like other proletarians; they lost their work and earnings when some producer could not find buyers for his goods. They worked for the lowest wages. When they tried to unite with organized labour they were often rejected as undesirable competitors with too low a standard of living. However black and white labourers may be separated or united, nevertheless their interests in general are the same, and often they are still fighting the same foe.

When the Dutch and the English sailed out with their large fleets, with new arms, with new theories and far-reaching plans, to come to blows with the Spaniards and the Portuguese, they attacked another world unity which claimed to be the true successor of the Roman Empire: the Catholic Church. The Catholic, "all-embracing" Church was the large body that united the conglomeration of states in the Middle Ages. As head of this Church, the pope had not only to decide on the fate of human souls. He exacted obedience from Christian rulers in all matters.

The Catholic Church was a centre of civilization. It promoted progress in agriculture, and in a great many countries it was the only organizer of scientific work in the Middle Ages. All philosophies and the ancient classic authors were studied within the Church. The Latin language, the language of the Church, was the one scientific language of all Christian nations. Students and teachers of different nations met at the universities. Scholars travelling from university to university unified human thinking. The Catholic Church created a common basis of music. The Gregorian chant took the place of the multiplicity of scales used in folk-song. The scholars moved in an atmosphere of unity though their brothers might be fighting in opposing armies. Yet even the soil their feet touched was the subject of dispute.

The pope instigated the crusades and decided which of the newly discovered regions were to be added to the possessions of which crown. The last decision of world dimensions was the division of the earth between the Spanish and Portuguese conquerors in 1493 by Pope Alexander VI.

Division of the Earth by the Pope

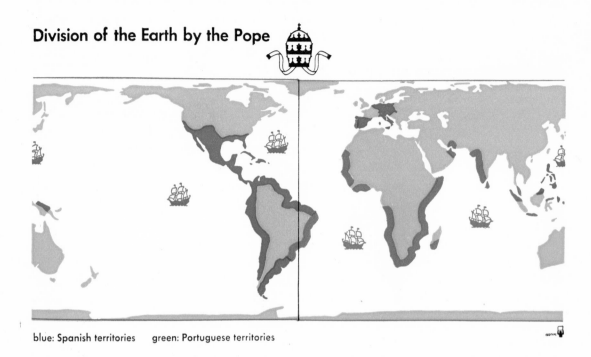

blue: Spanish territories   green: Portuguese territories

About a century later both empires were united for sixty years. They governed, according to the decision of the pope, the whole extra-European world which they had discovered and the oceans. And this gigantic realm existed in imagination only. At this moment other European forces were ripe to destroy the Spanish-Catholic unity of conquest and missions. Many European countries made discoveries and conquests, and the predominance of the Iberian peninsula vanished. The idea of one all-embracing Catholic Church disappeared for diplomats and men in the street, but not for the ruling groups of the Church itself. In principle the whole world is still a domain of the pope: in all countries there are bishoprics, and every square mile belongs to a province of the Church. A schism split the Church into two parts: the Roman-Latin-German territory in the west and the Greek-Slavic territory in the east. The Catholic Church was a centralized body, while the Orthodox churches were independent. The Patriarch of Constantinople was only *"primus inter pares."* Later the Reformation split the Roman Catholic Church: one part constituting the remaining Roman Catholic Church, and the rest composed of different "Protestant" bodies: Calvinists, Lutherans, Anglicans, and other groups. Thus the world power of the Catholic Church dwindled.

The former ideal unity—one pope, one religion, one emperor, one colonial empire—crashed. The present picture of the world bears no resemblance to this old centralized conception.

The Modern Division of the Earth

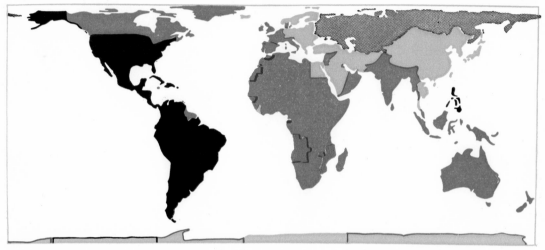

black: free American states, formerly partly European possessions
red: British Commonwealth of Nations, French, Italian, Dutch, Belgian, Danish territories

blue: Spanish territories
green: Portuguese territories
dark grey: Soviet Union

ISOTYPE

A bird's-eye view reveals: (1) formerly dependent regions which have freed themselves: the Latin American states from Spain and Portugal; the United States from England; (2) the Russian territories as the biggest continental entity; (3) the old states of eastern Asia which have resisted the white invasion; and a group of states in Asia and Europe not connected with modern conquests (or which have lost former extra-European territories, such as Germany and Sweden); and (4) western European countries which were the heirs of the former possessions of Spain and Portugal, leaving only small residues in Africa, (5) Spain, and (6) Portugal.

How was power transferred from the south to the north? How did the Mediterranean lose its significance? Why did the European minds turn from Mohammedan, Arabian, and Turkish problems to others peculiarly Western? Why did the maritime commerce of Genoa and Venice come to an end? A new type of conqueror arose in the north: the militant merchant, a type far superior to the militant missionary. He was backed by more aggressive groups: rich upstarts who produced goods for all the world. The new economic order developed first where the authority of the pope was resisted. Still based on Scholasticism, but freed from ecclesiastical prohibitions, science developed in all fields, improving techniques of production and navigation, establishing new laws and customs and state organizations, opening new vistas of power and success.

From the moment that the Atlantic became a connecting bridge and ceased to be a barrier, all the nations of the Atlantic coast of Europe assumed new and important positions:

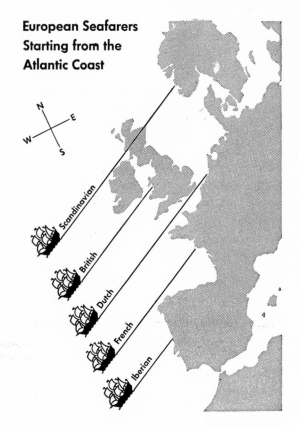

European Seafarers Starting from the Atlantic Coast

The Mediterranean Sea was relegated to the background. Venice and Genoa were at a disadvantage as competitors because of the somewhat longer voyage their vessels had to make.

Dutchmen and Englishmen attacked the Iberian Catholic empires where they were weakest. They built large fleets and destroyed the Iberian maritime supremacy. The Netherlands were far advanced. As early as 1500 their towns were great and powerful, comparable only with those of Italy, with which they were in manifold contact. The Dutch art of that time testifies to this binational intercourse. The towns bear witness to Dutch supremacy over the nations around the North Sea.

The Dutch held their position up to the eighteenth century, by which time the English had united and developed their stronger forces. About 1700 the Dutch fleet was the largest in the world. Dutch ships went to America, where the Dutch founded New Amsterdam, which later became English and was renamed New York. The Dutch voyaged to India, the Malay archipelago, China, and Japan, but as merchants, not as prophets. At their side the British and French began their commercial penetration of Asia. Like the Dutch, they started as traders. Conquest was the second step. Fighting merchants occupied great areas of India before governmental forces came into action. Commercial corporations with administrative powers formed the backbone of European expansion, especially of the British Empire. As late as the last few years of the nineteenth century British companies fought the natives with their own forces, aided by Imperial troops in emergencies. A part of the tradition of present-day governments is commercial. The Opium War was fought for purely commercial reasons; the Congo territory was first a private enterprise of the King of Belgium. In supporting commerce present-day governments merely follow tradition.

The evolution of the states which were in competition with Spain and Portugal was furthered not only by commercial predecessors of governmental institutions but also by groups of adventurers and pirates, some of them glowing with patriotism. Such permanent organizations, partly illegal, partly tolerated and secretly supported by governments, are of importance in human history. Roman generals had to fight pirates in great wars. In later centuries there were buccaneers of Saracen, British, French, Dutch, Spanish, and Portuguese origin, and the Barbary pirates of North Africa infested the Mediterranean up to a century ago. The freebooters of the seventeenth century organized a permanent naval force which harried the Caribbean Sea and Central America, and aided in destroying the Spanish and Portuguese monopoly as well as that of the Catholic Church—to the great satisfaction of the Dutch and the British.

The British Empire, transformed into the British Commonwealth of Nations, is a new type of world imperium, in a period of increasing centralization of internal and external power. Pan-Americanism tends to develop in a similar direction. Perhaps this is a characteristic of modernity in its infancy.

If we adhere to the view that tradition and old conditioned reactions are essential in human organization, it is fair to ask: What are British traditions? In Roman times the inhabitants of the British Isles were not good sailors. Scandinavian invaders who ultimately became their rulers taught them sailing, but also much more: the Norsemen may be regarded as the creators of a new type of empire.

Norse war-lords and their followers did not establish a real state community. They went to those countries where they found the most wealth and the least resistance. Norsemen came to Novgorod (Holmgard) and Constantinople (Mikligard), to Iceland and Vinland (probably as far as Boston), to France (Normandy) and Sicily in the ninth, tenth, and eleventh centuries. All these groups together, including vassals and servants of different birth, constituted a certain national complex. Norsemen established permanent communities in Normandy in the tenth and eleventh centuries, and in Sicily in the eleventh century served as auxiliary troops and bodyguards for different knights and kings. In this capacity they may have had to fight one another occasionally. The communities of Norsemen often came to one another's aid when they were in military difficulties. Co-operation between independent groups was characteristic of them. We know of treaties made by Norsemen; on their side a series of names appears, on the other side but one name, as the representative of a great empire.

Vikings

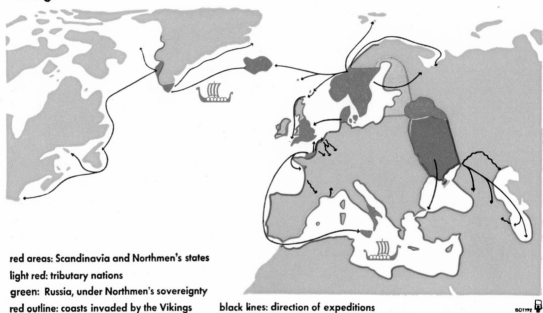

red areas: Scandinavia and Northmen's states
light red: tributary nations
green: Russia, under Northmen's sovereignty
red outline: coasts invaded by the Vikings   black lines: direction of expeditions

This was the Norsemen's nationality and influence.

The Norse sea-kings became land-kings with court and country. In England a "Vikingization" began, and the English people, an amalgamation of different bloods, went to sea as the Vikings had done before them, influenced perhaps by Viking tradition. Co-operation between independent groups became a British characteristic after periods of fighting and exploitation. Probably Anglo-Saxons forced a great many people to learn that co-operation is unavoidable among groups which had once been enemies. The one great loss that the British Empire sustained was the colonies that are now the United States, and that loss must be attributed to a temporary lack of co-operation within the ruling classes in Great Britain. Further losses by emigration of the English and Irish population, and the persistence of the Irish question, are to be similarly explained. But these experiences were not wasted: the changes that took place, especially during the last few decades, are remarkable. On the Treaty of Versailles a series of names appears representing the British Empire: those of the delegates of all dominions and other British territories. According to the Statute of Westminster passed by the House of Commons in 1931, "every self-governing member of the Empire is master of its destiny" and the Dominions are "autonomous communities within the British Empire and freely associated." This is the British Commonwealth of Nations:

British Expansion

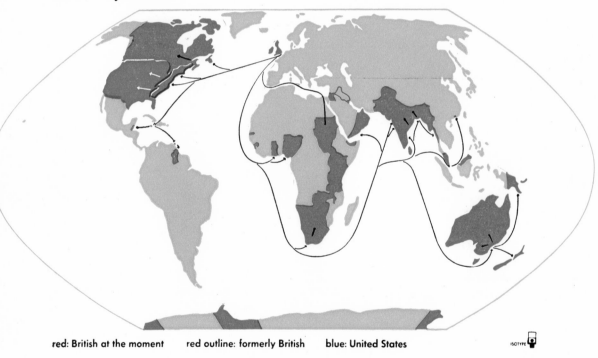

red: British at the moment   red outline: formerly British   blue: United States

British expansion was like that of the Vikings, but on a larger scale. More people emigrated to foreign countries. It seems that many Vikings left Scandinavia because they had conflicts with the governor and preferred a free life abroad to one of oppression at home. So, too, the Britons. Many of the emigrants were political or religious refugees; some were criminals—for example, many of those who were sent to Australia. Nevertheless most of them retained their nationality and dependency

41

on the mother country, more even than the Vikings, who left their country in youth, when political organizations were in the making, and sometimes returned in old age. The spread of Britons over the whole earth, the spread of the English language as an international means of communication, contributed much to the unification of mankind.

Trends Towards Modernity

Urbanization, Births and Deaths

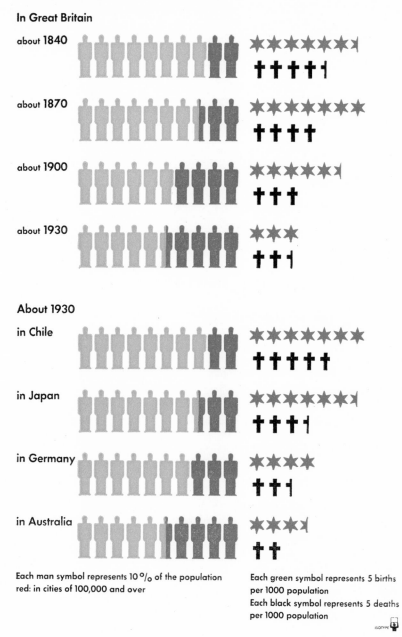

In Great Britain

about 1840

about 1870

about 1900

about 1930

About 1930

in Chile

in Japan

in Germany

in Australia

Each man symbol represents 10 % of the population
red: in cities of 100,000 and over

Each green symbol represents 5 births
per 1000 population

Each black symbol represents 5 deaths
per 1000 population

Urbanization is a characteristic of modernity.

Chile is, roughly speaking, at the stage at which England was a hundred years ago, and Australia is as well off as England is today. Urbanization brings about many changes in the life of modern men. The drop in death-rates tells the story of modern public health organization and of health education in general. Nations have learned to control not only the plague but also cholera, tuberculosis, syphilis, and other infectious diseases. The rational method of combating death is the result of social behaviour based on the application of science, on the attempt to anticipate and control events. Typical of this trend is the spread of birth-control and hence of a decreasing birth-rate all over the world.

Birth-Rates
in a Central European Town

1591	🚼🚼🚼🚼
1599	🚼🚼🚼🚼🚼🚼
1624	🚼🚼🚼🚼🚼
1626	🚼🚼🚼🚼🚼🚼
1656	🚼🚼🚼🚼🚼🚼🚼
1657	🚼🚼🚼🚼🚼
1783	🚼🚼🚼
1830	🚼🚼🚼
1880	🚼🚼🚼🚼
1900	🚼🚼🚼
1913	🚼🚼
1918 War	🚼
1930	🚼

Each symbol represents 1 birth per 100 population

In spite of a decreasing birth-rate, populations have tended to grow in our time. The world might be divided into three regions: the Western world, including both Americas, Europe, and the Soviet Union (white area and white man symbols); the Far East, including China, Japan, and their dependencies, such as Tibet (grey area and grey man symbols); and the Southern world, including Africa, the Near and Middle East, with India and the Malay archipelago, the islands of the southern Pacific, and Australia (black area and black man symbols). It may be asked whether the growth of population is particularly confined to one of these regions; the answer is no:

46

The Growth of Mankind

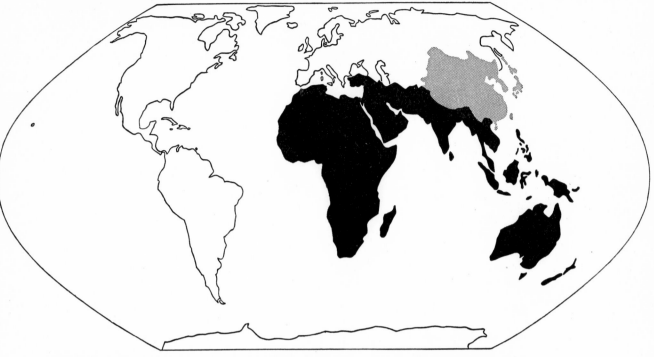

white: the two Americas, Europe, the Soviet Union   grey: region of Chinese and Japanese population
black: other parts of the world

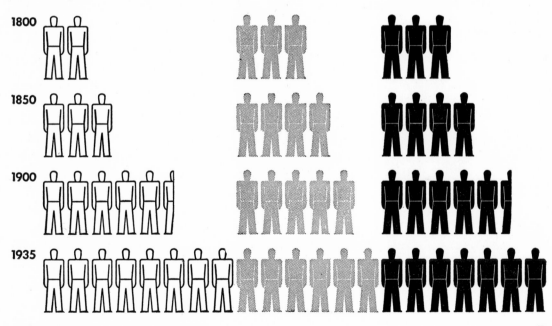

1800

1850

1900

1935

Each symbol represents 100 million men

47

An intense growth of population is common to these three regions despite their differences in economic and technical development. When "technical development" or "mechanization" by the use of coal, petroleum, and water-power is visualized, we have this distribution of mechanization:

Mechanization of the World

America, Europe, Soviet Union

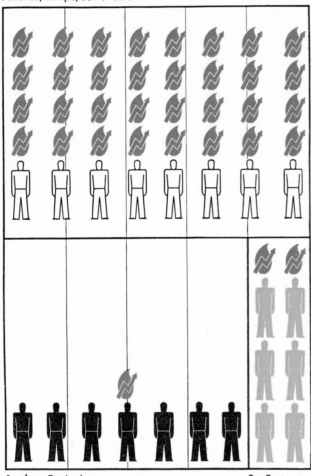

Southern Territories   Far East

Each rectangle represents 5 million square miles
Each man symbol represents 100 million population
Each red symbol represents 50,000 million kilowatt hours
produced annually from coal, petroleum and water-power

The differences are very great, despite the backwardness of such Western countries as Latin America and the Soviet Union. The same is true of the density of population: To the regions of high density—Europe, India, central China—vast empty regions have been added, especially in Europe and India.

48

If we select single countries—for instance, all the countries of about twenty million inhabitants and over—the differences are even greater:

Power Used per Capita in 1936

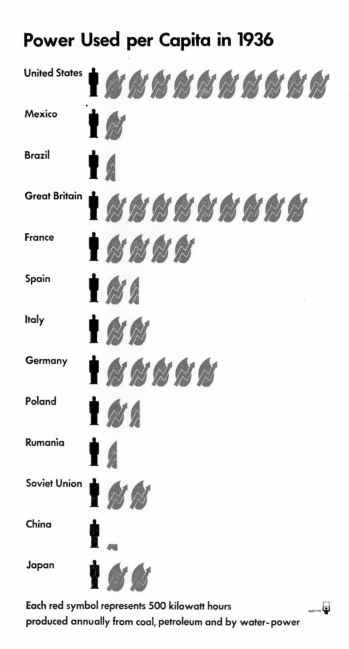

Each red symbol represents 500 kilowatt hours
produced annually from coal, petroleum and by water-power

Fuel is partly used to produce heat by combustion, and not only for power. To a large extent, power is used for expanding the apparatus of production or in preparation for war. Though our chart cannot give more than a rough idea, nevertheless it shows a common attribute of the so-called "Big Seven": the United States, Great Britain, France, Italy, Germany, the Soviet Union, and Japan. All of these use 1000 kilowatt-hours or more per inhabitant annually. This might lead to the conclusion that a state of about twenty millions and over must reach a certain technological level if it is to exercise any international influence of importance. The highest technological level accompanies the highest level of living-conditions.

A considerable part of the power in the United States is used in automobiles. Great differences in power-consumption between countries may be explained by showing the number of automobiles used:

Automobiles per 200 Population

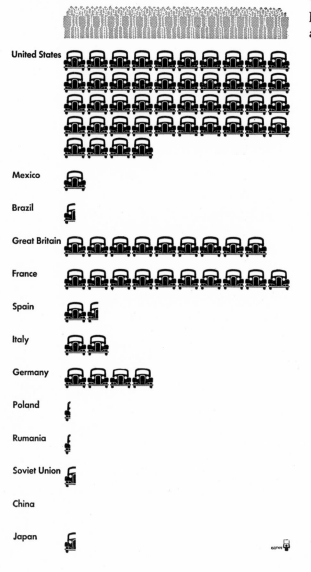

United States

Mexico

Brazil

Great Britain

France

Spain

Italy

Germany

Poland

Rumania

Soviet Union

China

Japan

50

The number of "robots" working for man is growing more rapidly than the population. Mechanization in manufacture is increasing in all countries in spite of the fact that economic depressions and other social factors hinder or prevent the full use of all natural resources and technical equipment.

Horse-Power Used in Manufacturing Industries. United States

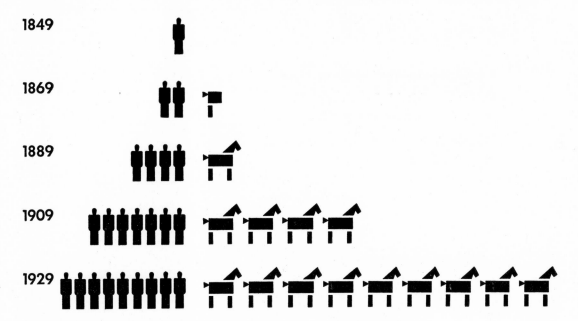

1849
1869
1889
1909
1929

Each man symbol represents 1 million wage-earners in manufacturing industries
Each horse symbol represents 5 million horse-power

ISOTYPE

All this machinery is mostly used 40 to 48 hours weekly. Actually it could be used 100 or 120 hours weekly and be of more benefit. Though not used to their full capacity, machines have caused an enormous growth in production and consumption which might improve still further the living-conditions of mankind. The same is true of agriculture. Today much less human labour is necessary to produce food for human consumption. This is one reason why the proportion of rural population to urban may decrease without imperilling the general food-supply. The "iron horse" has become the farmer's best friend:

10924

Horse-Power Used in Agriculture. United States

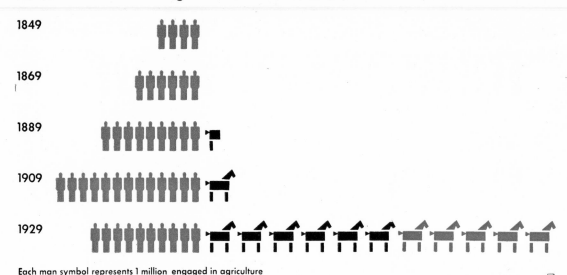

Each man symbol represents 1 million engaged in agriculture
Each horse symbol represents 5 million horse-power   black: machinery   blue: trucks

The technological progress of agriculture which has contributed to make the growth of population in all parts of the world possible began before the industrial revolution reached the Southern and Eastern world. The Chinese developed methods of intensive use of the soil centuries ago. Long ago they learned to fertilize their plants systematically, but without developing natural sciences. Neither India nor the Europe of the pre-industrial age reached this level; the European peasant had to be taught by scientists to adopt new methods of feeding the soil. For the Western world fertilizing is a modern scientific advance; for the Eastern world it is traditional. The mechanization of agriculture did not make much progress in the Eastern world where single plants and combinations of crops were cultivated by hand. Tractors, combines, and similar machines can be used only on large tracts.

The growing western mechanization changed the whole of life, especially the worker's life. Weaving, for instance, was formerly carried on in the workers' homes, wives and children doing their share. When men, women, and children had to go into the factory for long working days, production increased, but home life of the old type was destroyed.

52

Home and Factory Weaving in England

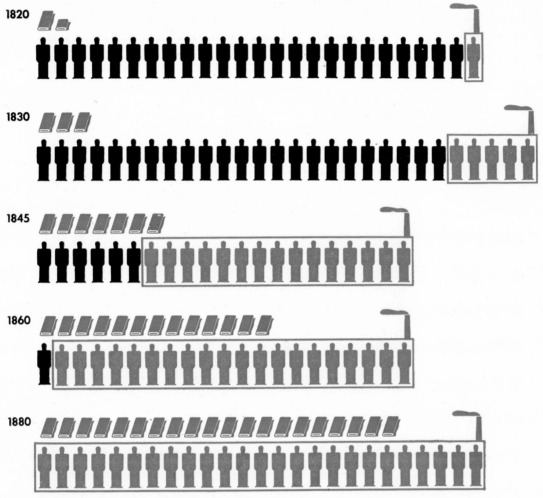

1820

1830

1845

1860

1880

Each blue symbol represents 50 million pounds total production
Each black man symbol represents 10,000 home weavers
Each red man symbol represents 10,000 factory weavers

By this separation of home and place of work the burden of labour grew much heavier. Moreover, the industrial revolution started by lengthening the working time; machinery created a new type of oppression instead of freeing men from the necessity of long hours of slow hand-work. The machine, which should be the best friend of man, seemed to be his enemy. The workers often destroyed the machines which made them work eighteen hours a day or not at all, leaving them unemployed

53

and without bread. After decades of such disturbances in all countries, working-conditions improved. Child labour was abolished in most parts of the Western world, female labour was reduced, working hours were shortened. A new life, with more leisure, began. More leisure means a richer personal life, and therefore a happier one, according to modern ideas.

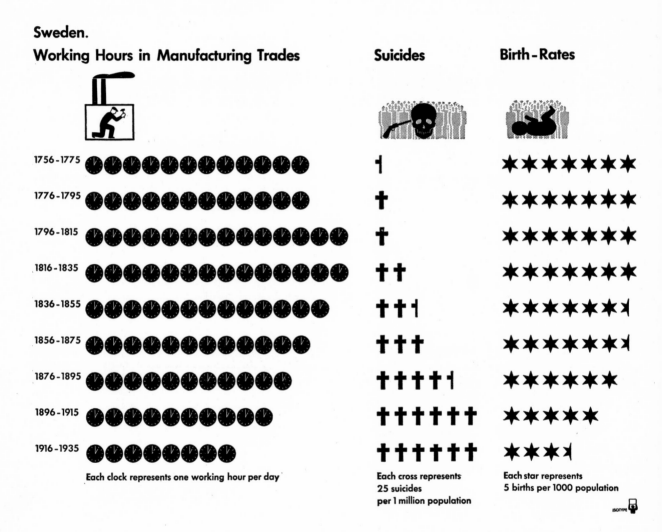

Sweden.

Working Hours in Manufacturing Trades   **Suicides**   **Birth-Rates**

Each clock represents one working hour per day

Each cross represents 25 suicides per 1 million population

Each star represents 5 births per 1000 population

Customs and tradition were altered by collective work in factories and offices, by the expansion of rational activities, by the wide circulation of newspapers, books, and other modern means of communication, which rapidly reduced the number of illiterates. These changes cannot all be depicted statistically. Still, it is possible to answer some questions indirectly. What part, for instance, does religion play in the life of our time? The increase of the suicide-rate and the decrease of the birth-rate may be regarded as signs of the weakening influence of the Church. Both suicide and birth-control were forbidden by many Christian communities, and still are.

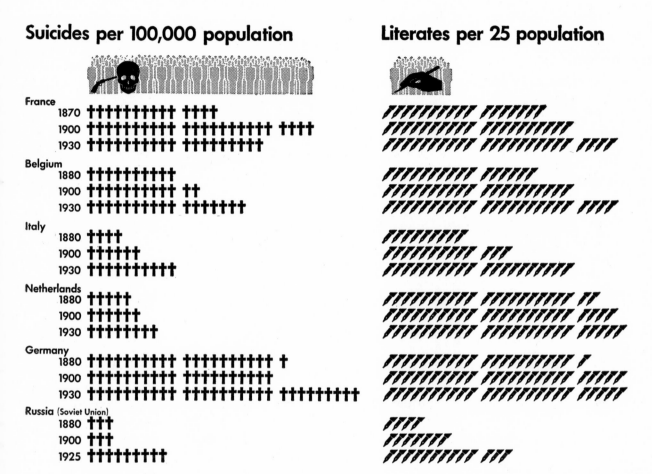

Suicides per 100,000 population

Literates per 25 population

France
1870
1900
1930

Belgium
1880
1900
1930

Italy
1880
1900
1930

Netherlands
1880
1900
1930

Germany
1880
1900
1930

Russia (Soviet Union)
1880
1900
1925

The number of suicides cannot be used as a measure of unhappiness. Despite the horror and anguish of the World War, the suicide-rate decreased. It turns out that suicide is not a major cause of death and that its continuous increase hardly influences the falling death-rate. Nevertheless the increase in the suicide-rate is an important symptom of modernity. Two centuries ago philosophers hesitated to speak freely about suicide. Now the trend to self-destruction is common to all Christian nations, though very remarkable differences can be shown between various countries and groups of different Christian faith.

Assuming that the death of relatives and friends brings sorrow and that the loss of children makes parents unhappy, it must be agreed that the causes of unhappiness are decreasing in spite of the increase in the suicide-rate. The history of a family of two hundred years ago is very different from the history of a modern family:

Four Generations of a Family

in the seventeenth century   **in the nineteenth century**

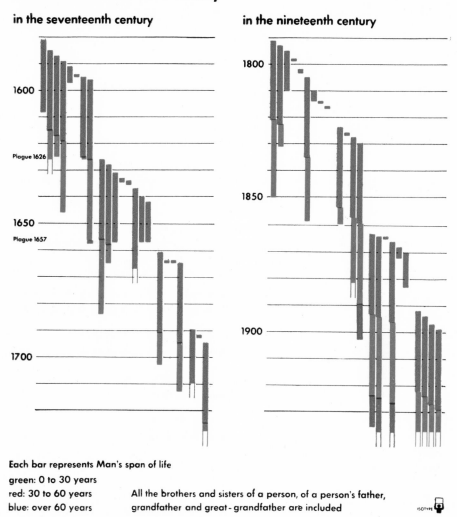

Each bar represents Man's span of life
green: 0 to 30 years
red: 30 to 60 years   All the brothers and sisters of a person, of a person's father,
blue: over 60 years   grandfather and great-grandfather are included   ISOTYPE

Here a particular family has been selected in which the number of births did not decrease excessively, so as to show how much less frequently the death of a relative shocks now than formerly. Centuries ago it happened more than once that members of the same family died in the same year of the plague (for instance, the plague of 1657) or some other epidemic.

56

We must realize to what extent unhappiness caused by death has changed. In this special case no child in the last generation died; but the average life-span was already lengthening in earlier generations. The most striking difference is that formerly not a single member of this particular family reached the age of sixty. Men, too, died earlier. It should be mentioned that several who survived after 1930 had been soldiers in the World War.

That infants survive is quite the rule now; their death has become an exception. Here are typical examples of the trend of infant mortality:

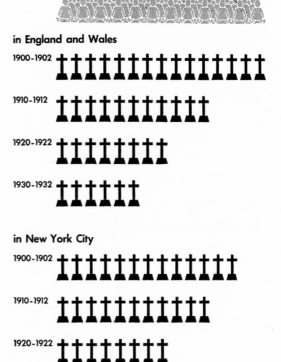

Infant Deaths per 100 Births

in England and Wales

1900-1902

1910-1912

1920-1922

1930-1932

in New York City

1900-1902

1910-1912

1920-1922

1930-1932

The decrease in birth-rate and in infant mortality, the increase in literacy and in suicide-rate, the increase in mechanization and in urbanization may be regarded as signs of modernity. These Western trends do not depend upon any particular social and political order; they are found in the United States and in the Soviet Union, in France and in Germany.

Because of lower birth- and death-rates, the "trees of population" tend to develop a larger "crown." Successive generations may expect to overlap for a long time:

Age Groups in England and Wales

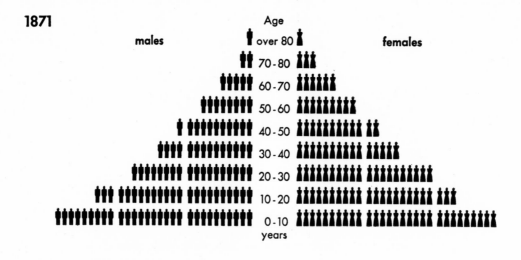

1871

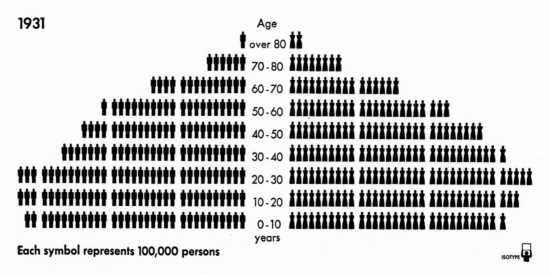

1931

Each symbol represents 100,000 persons

Should modern men be able to apply scientific management to production and distribution, many retired people would be able to live on pensions granted by the government. This would involve no lengthening of working hours, but a systematic use of all our scientific knowledge, technical devices, and natural resources. There would be no such anomalies as the destruction of coffee or restriction in the production of cotton and other goods.

58

The trend of modernity is towards longer life and increasing technical equipment. Good plumbing is found in many homes. The use of automobiles, telephones, and radios is general. Some countries introduce one technical innovation, others another. In the Soviet Union, for instance, telephones were in general use before bathtubs. In Germany they are more common than automobiles; in France the reverse is true.

Telephones and Automobiles per 200 Population

France

Germany

If a country is "modern" in one field, it is not necessarily "modern" in all the others. A general or average "index of modernity" conceals certain peculiarities which are important not only in technologically appraising single countries but in understanding the whole process of modernization, which is the subject of this survey.

Certain qualities are so closely correlated with others that one serves to characterize the whole group. If there is a very high rate of mortality in a country, the rate of morbidity or the birth-rate is not likely to be extremely low. Therefore, if we try to arrange nations according to two grades of death-rate we arrive generally at the same result as if we arrange them according to two grades of birth-rate:

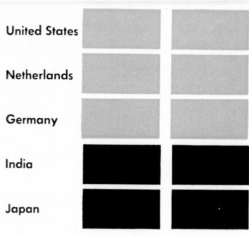

Death - Rate   Birth - Rate

	Death - Rate	Birth - Rate
United States		
Netherlands		
Germany		
India		
Japan		

Death-rate   grey: below 15°/oo
              black: above 15°/oo

Birth-rate   grey: below 25°/oo
              black: above 25°/oo

No such correlation is found in degrees of mechanization or urbanization or the waning influence of Church and custom, though both trends are parallel. The suicide-rate might be used as evidence of the Church's decline, if we bear in mind the anti-suicide tradition in Christian nations and the pro-suicide tradition in Japan, especially in the ruling classes:

Even in Christian nations few suicides may correspond with a high degree of mechanization. In the Netherlands, with its strong religious traditions and family life, the suicide-rate is low, but mechanization is high.

Silhouettes, which are simplified integrations of various qualities, bring out the different features of different nations and the degree of modernization of various groups.

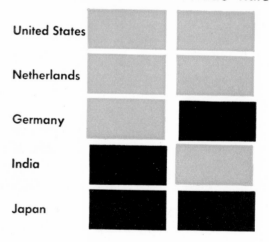

Death - Rate   Suicide - Rate

	Death - Rate	Suicide - Rate
United States		
Netherlands		
Germany		
India		
Japan		

Death-rate   grey: below 15°/oo
               black: above 15°/oo

Suicide-rate   grey: below 2°/ooo
               black: above 2°/ooo

60

Silhouettes

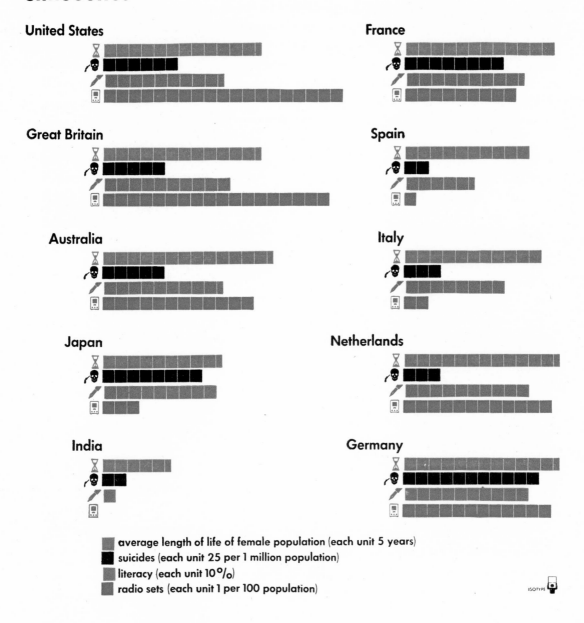

United States

France

Great Britain

Spain

Australia

Italy

Japan

Netherlands

India

Germany

- average length of life of female population (each unit 5 years)
- suicides (each unit 25 per 1 million population)
- literacy (each unit 10%)
- radio sets (each unit 1 per 100 population)

ISOTYPE

Some countries are very similar. For instance, Italy and Spain, or the United States and Great Britain. But Mexico is of the Spanish type and on a lower level. Germany would resemble the Netherlands very much (see the silhouettes above), were it not for the suicide-rate, expressing the vigour of different traditions.

61

These silhouettes are very incomplete. They do not show the degree of personal freedom in a society, and other factors, but they do show a great many facts. It is possible to imagine that the life-span could be lengthened in other countries to the degree that it has been lengthened in Australia and that it will be so lengthened in the near future, but it is impossible to imagine exactly how we can control the secretions of the glands of the human body and thus prolong youth. Nor is it possible to imagine the social consequences of such control. Would there be a struggle for glands and hormones as there is now a struggle for wealth?

The effect of using technological aids in our daily life and of reducing working hours can be foreseen, but not the changes caused by cosmic rays and other extra-terrestrial influences.

Granting a trend towards longer life and more leisure, is there an international trend towards eliminating the insecurity of living-conditions? Is there any sign that war will be abolished or internal restlessness alleviated? Or of cherishing and expanding freedom of expression and scientific thought and action?

State of the World

Man's daily life, his happiness and unhappiness, depends upon old and new customs and institutions, upon a great many agencies. The modernity of living-conditions depends, first of all, upon technical equipment and natural resources. A bird's-eye view of the interconnexions between all parts of a society in action makes it possible to analyse the state of the world or the structure of a single country. The general scheme remains the same:

Economic Scheme

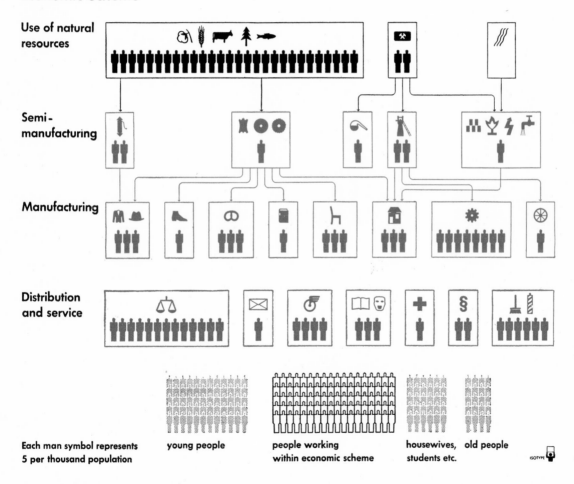

Each man symbol represents 5 per thousand population   young people   people working within economic scheme   housewives, students etc.   old people

Such a scheme leads to the question: How is it possible to increase the production of food and drink, shelter and recreation, the building of houses, schools, and theatres and to reduce working hours, the number of accidents, disease, and other burdens? Examination of such a question may be begun with purely technical facts without regarding the social structure which is the basis of all human actions.

The different regions of the world provide different raw materials, such as: pig iron (Fe = ferrum), rubber, cotton, wool, linen, rayon, and silk.

Raw Materials

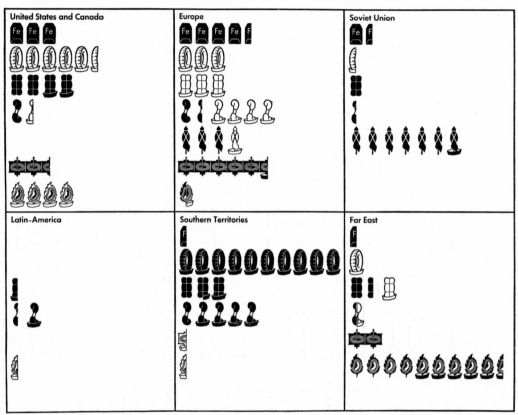

Each full coloured symbol represents 10% of world production   on ship: exported   outlined, on white ship: imported
pig iron, rubber, cotton, wool, linen, rayon, silk

This rough scheme distinguishes six great regions: (1) the United States and Canada, with their predominantly English-speaking population; (2) Latin America, a group of similar nations; (3) Europe without the Soviet Union; (4) the Soviet Union; (5) the Far East, composed of China and Japan; (6) the Southern territories, containing Africa, the Near and Middle East, southern Asia, and Australia. Most of the raw materials produced in this Southern world are used by the Western countries. In spite of all artificially produced substitutes Western industrial centres cannot be expected to achieve self-sufficiency in raw materials in the near future.

Food and Drink

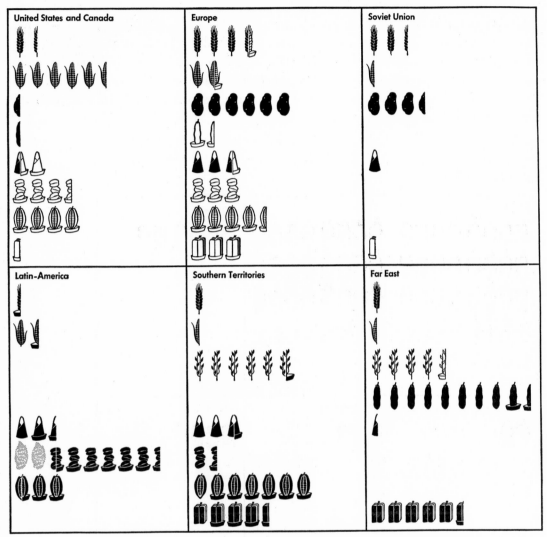

Each full coloured symbol represents 10% of world production   on ship: exported   outlined, on white ship: imported

wheat and rye, corn, rice, potatoes, soy beans, sugar, coffee, cocoa, tea

These two schemes tell the story of many important conflicts. Rubber comes from the Southern world. The United States must buy rubber abroad, and especially from British and Dutch territories. It has made desperate efforts to renovate used rubber and to produce substitutes for rubber synthetically. The Southern world has to provide the Western world with much raw material for industrial centres and with many foodstuffs, leaving the masses of population in the South on a low subsistence level. Not only the ruling classes, but also the workers of Anglo-Saxon America and of Europe participate in these benefits, paid for by the Southern workers.

Degrees of industrialization can be gauged by the amount of coal and petroleum used for producing heat and power and the amount of water-power used for generating electricity. With the actual power, produced by coal, petroleum, and water, is shown the potential energy which could be generated by running water. There are great reserves in the Southern world. There are also great resources of coal and petroleum underground in the Soviet Union, which is beginning to develop their possibilities and which may before long assume a commanding industrial position among the nations of the world.

Sources of Power

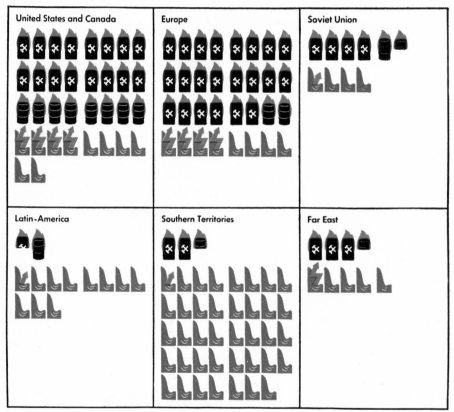

Each symbol represents 25,000 million kilowatt hours produced annually

sources of power: coal, petroleum, water with lightning-flash: being used

What is true of single countries is also true of larger regions of the world: A wider use of power is an indication of increasing modernity, and is connected with a higher urbanization, which is in turn an indication of modernity.

The two are closely related:

Population

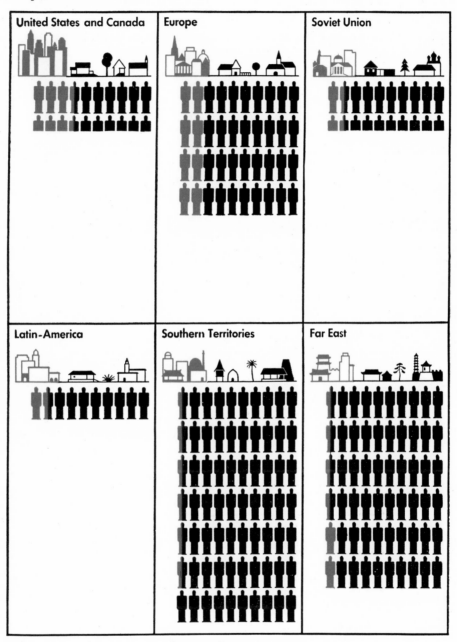

Each man symbol represents 10 million population   red: in cities of 100,000 population and more

ISOTYPE

Subsistence levels vary. The highest is to be found in Anglo-Saxon countries, such as England, the United States, Australia, and New Zealand. This is a standard for the white population, though not all British subjects reach it. The standard of the Hindu population of India is actually not much higher than that of the Chinese. The situation around the Pacific is not unique. Contiguous countries have different subsistence standards, the better-off maintaining theirs by closing their frontiers to the immigration of cheap labour. One way of judging subsistence levels is to picture the consumption of sugar per inhabitant.

Annual Sugar Consumption per Head in Countries around the Pacific

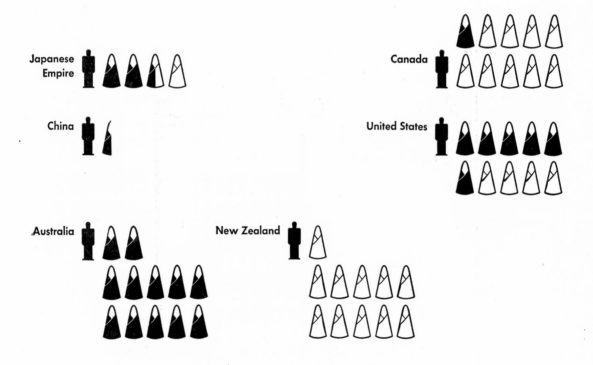

Each symbol represents 10 pounds of sugar
black: home production   white: imported

70

It is a matter of fact that precisely those countries with a high subsistence level can feed a much larger population with the products of their soil, without lowering the standard, and that those with a low level cannot do much more than extract a livelihood from the soil.

Compare the actual population with the potential population—that is, the population which might be fed with the products of the native soil, produced by present technical means—and a new type of density is obtained. Countries may be divided into overcrowded, crowded, and more or less empty ones. Japan proper depends partly upon imports. China produces no surplus food.

Area per Head in Countries around the Pacific

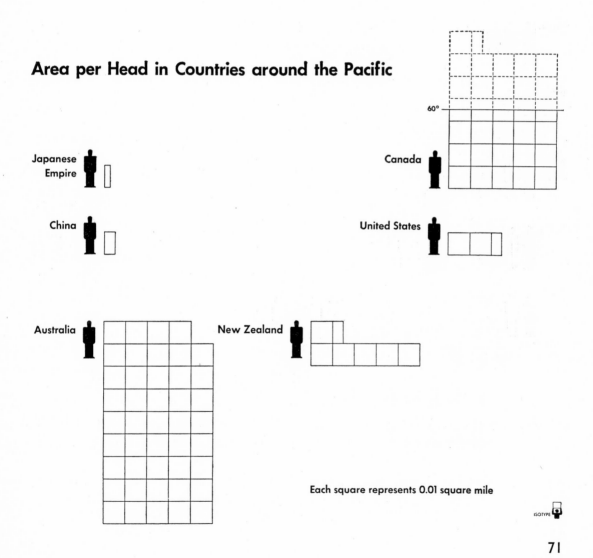

Each square represents 0.01 square mile

Before general measures were taken to prevent them, there were considerable dislocations of population. Many Chinese left their country when there was a famine. Many Japanese migrated because of overcrowding. The result is clearly visible in the change of the population of Hawaii, which had suffered great loss from infectious diseases which were imported from Europe, but which are not usually fatal to Europeans, who have acquired a certain immunity to them.

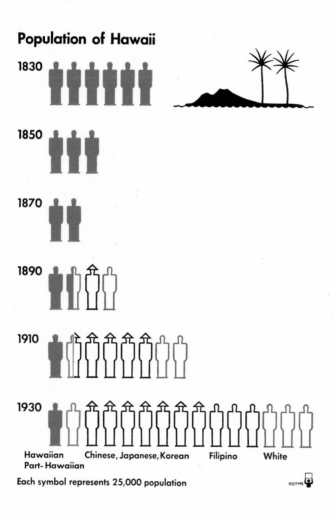

Population of Hawaii

1830

1850

1870

1890

1910

1930

Hawaiian
Part-Hawaiian

Chinese, Japanese, Korean

Filipino

White

Each symbol represents 25,000 population

Despite many regulatory laws, migration is not yet the subject of international planning. Sometimes people are forced to go to foreign countries. Armenians had to leave Turkey in masses. Jews have been driven out of central European countries. Sometimes want forces the underprivileged to seek work and food in foreign countries, as East Indians did in South Africa and South America. Sometimes immigration is forbidden or limited. There is no economics of humanity.

72

Immigration in the United States is closely related to the entire economic situation, especially to the production of iron up to the World War.

United States. Annual Iron-Production and Immigration

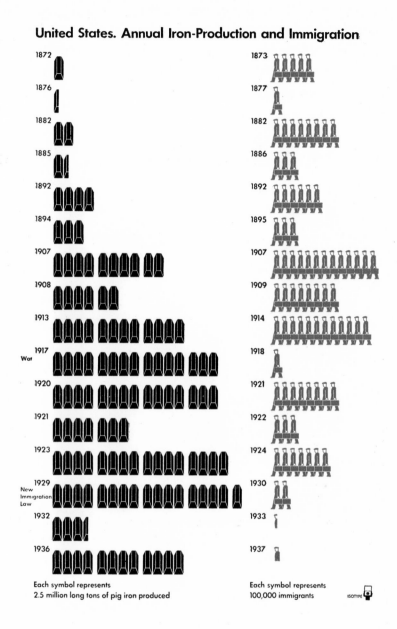

Each symbol represents
2.5 million long tons of pig iron produced

Each symbol represents
100,000 immigrants

ISOTYPE

In the last few decades emigration for political reasons from the Soviet Union, Turkey, Germany, and Italy was more pronounced than during earlier times. Now hundreds of thousands of expatriates live in foreign countries.

Only the Soviet Union has been free from depressions and shown only an upward development in production, but it does not admit masses of immigrants. Planning excludes the type of economic crisis so well known in other countries. Fluctuations in production and consumption may also arise in the Soviet Union, but only because of special changes in organization or technical equipment. Business cycles, once more or less national, become more and more international. The great world depression affected all countries except the Soviet Union:

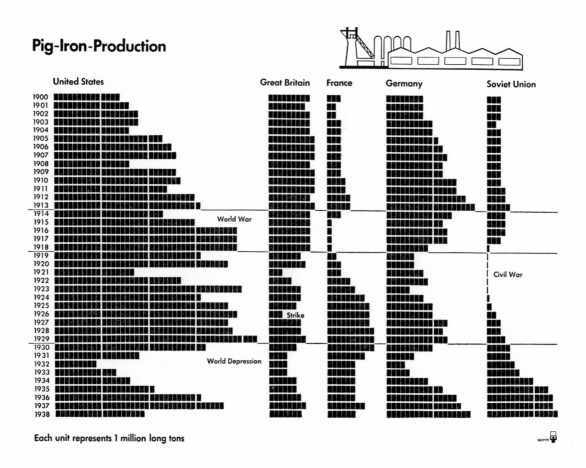

Pig-Iron-Production

United States   Great Britain   France   Germany   Soviet Union

Each unit represents 1 million long tons

Fluctuations depend not only upon business cycles but also upon other things. For instance, rearmament in one state may increase the production of raw materials in another. Sweden illustrates very well to what extent the situation in one country depends upon activities in another.

74

Exports of Iron Ore from Sweden

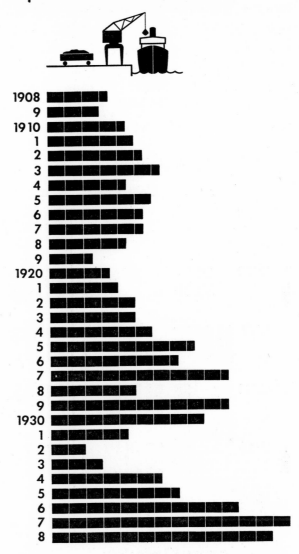

Each unit represents 1 million long tons

The influence of the World War is obvious: rapid pre-war development, insecurity at the outbreak of the war in 1914, the lack of orders corrected by a surplus of orders in 1915, a very stable export trade during the rest of the war (the most regular of all periods, though not the most prosperous), a slump after the war, a rapid but restless development till 1929, and, after a serious depression, a new turn for the better, which seems to be closely connected with the armament programs in other countries.

The present is a time of unrest and disturbance in production, of ups and downs in prices and wages, in profits and investments. Increasing profit leads bankers and manufacturers, farmers and explorers to make new investments; if the profit is doubtful, investing ceases. Upon this question of profit everything depends: investment or non-investment, production of more or less goods, employment or unemployment, high or low purchasing power, food or hunger, shelter or vagrancy, hope or fear. The tendency to reduce production—and also thereby to reduce consumption—as a measure to keep prices high is general:

World Cotton-Production

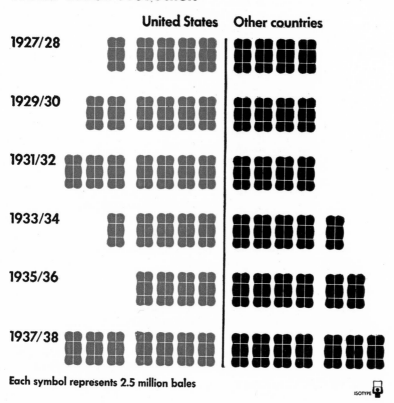

Each symbol represents 2.5 million bales

Even the acreage of cotton-fields was reduced in the United States by governmental intervention.

Not only restriction of production but also destruction plays its part: crops, mining, and oil-production are the subject of international agreements. Milk and grain have been destroyed in America, cocoa in Liberia, cattle in Denmark, vegetables in the Netherlands, coffee in Brazil. Destruction of machines, automobiles, ships takes place because they no longer pay and not because they are no longer fit to be used.

76

Market Regulation by Destruction, Brazil 1927-1937

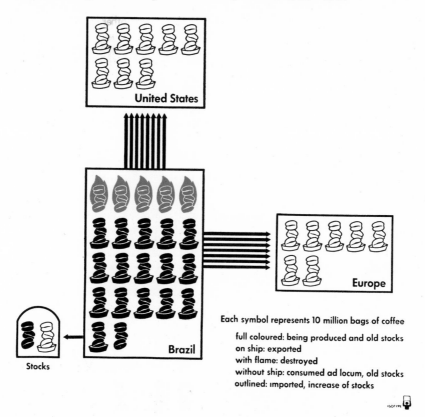

Each symbol represents 10 million bags of coffee

full coloured: being produced and old stocks
on ship: exported
with flame: destroyed
without ship: consumed ad locum, old stocks
outlined: imported, increase of stocks

The world production of coffee is concentrated chiefly in Latin America, especially in Brazil. Hence the conditions for planned destruction are those laid down in Brazil. The choice within the present social order lies between economic depression and bankruptcy on the one hand and planned destruction, with a possible loss of world status on the other. Destruction is provided for by law. It is not practised when war is imminent or when comprehensive planning is necessary to prepare for war, as in Italy and Germany. In these countries planning, control of raw material for import and export and for home use, goes hand in hand with profits.

Even in the Soviet Union, which has an economic system no longer depending on profit, a special kind of destruction may occur, such as the slaughtering of cattle in connexion with the collectivization of farms. But these are transition phenomena and not something inherent in the system. However, some think the phenomena are the consequences of some types of dictatorship and that they entail a combination of planning and liberty of decision. Man today is accustomed to destruction; but he knows that the possibilities of production and reconstruction are enormous. The rate at which ships were built after the World War shows what can be done:

77

Merchant Vessels Launched per Year

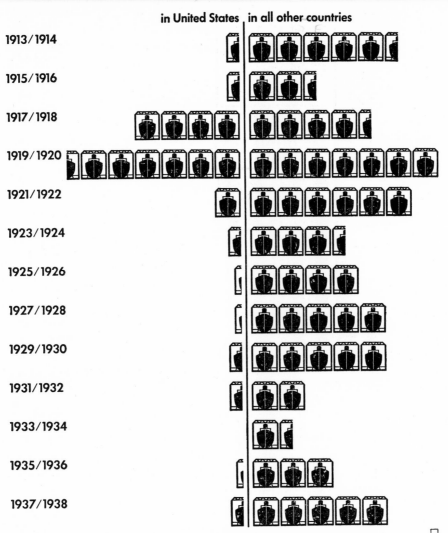

Each symbol represents 500,000 gross tons (Vessels of 100 gross tons and over)

ISOTYPE

During the World War many ships were lost, and comparatively few were built. The activity of the merchant marine was much reduced. Increasing postwar demands were fulfilled rapidly. Not only were losses made good, but the world's merchant marine grew, adapted to expanding world trade. Suddenly shipbuilding stopped again—not because countries needed no more goods, but because the profits of world trade decreased. If it were not necessary to have a certain reserve of ships for wartime—to serve as troop transports or as hospital ships, or, after modification, even as cruisers—many more would probably have been scrapped during the depression, to stem the rising tide of loss.

78

Cotton-production, coffee-production, and shipbuilding may flourish as before if the market situation is changed and buyers are in a position to spend money. Again, a new situation might arise, if the production basis has been changed. The present ups and downs are terrifying to many people—not only those who are directly affected, but also others who depend upon certain branches of this trade for profits. A nation which buys and sells in the international market is affected by all the international accidents which may occur. Many American wheat-growers, for instance, live by exporting their produce. This is what happened to the wheat exports of the United States:

United States, Wheat Trade

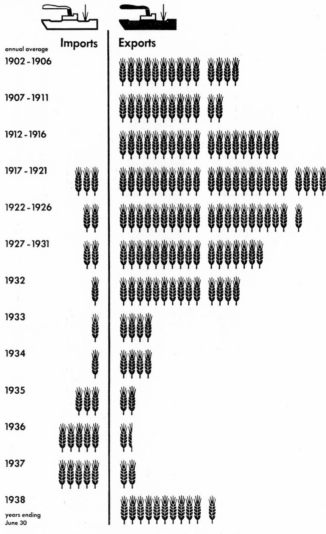

Each symbol represents 10 million bushels of wheat and flour
(flour expressed in corresponding quantity of grain)

ISOTYPE

79

The world situation has fundamentally changed in the last decade. Europe is on her way towards self-sufficiency:

Wheat Trade

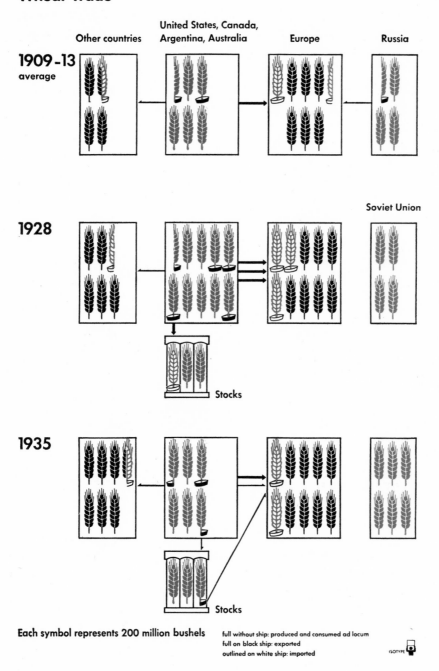

Each symbol represents 200 million bushels

full without ship: produced and consumed ad locum
full on black ship: exported
outlined on white ship: imported

ISOTYPE

"Autarchy"—self-sufficiency—not only destroys international connexions, but in industrial countries lowers the quality of products and the standard of living. Free trade always inclines to support production of one kind of goods and specialization. The "banana states" of Central America are examples. Specialization is responsible for differences in type and standard of living. Because of the trend towards self-sufficiency, the international division of labour is reduced. The effect is to make human life more uniform everywhere, despite isolation. The agrarian countries are forced to build up a manufacturing industry of their own when they find no buyers for their agricultural products. Lacking foreign credit, they can no longer trade with foreign countries. This new industrialization, which especially promotes the mechanization of agriculture, means an adaptation to the general level of the more advanced countries, not only in the field of methods of production, but also in the standard of living. Purely agrarian nations generally have a lower standard of living because the desire for bread is not elastic, and the possibility of increasing the production of food is limited. Manufactures have a much wider latitude; the use of radio sets, of automobiles, of typewriters may develop enormously.

The tendency towards increasing self-sufficiency parallels a decreasing world trade. This may be illustrated by the case of Europe:

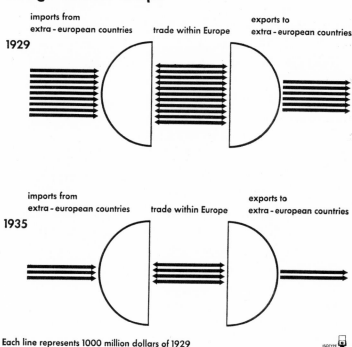

Foreign Trade in Europe

imports from
extra - european countries   trade within Europe   exports to
extra - european countries

1929

imports from
extra - european countries   trade within Europe   exports to
extra - european countries

1935

Each line represents 1000 million dollars of 1929

This is part of the international change in trade and production and is closely connected with preparations for war.

All these ups and downs characterize the situation, but it cannot be said that they characterize modernity. The number of people who want to bring about such fluctuations if they are non-existent is very small. Nobody thinks of "imitating" business fluctuations as plumbing and skyscrapers are imitated. It may happen that the Russians imitate Western people by producing "period furniture," Corinthian columns and capitals, but it is difficult to imagine their deliberately causing economic crises, periods of prosperity and depression. The people of our time try to overcome these shortcomings of an economic system. One country imitates another's way of resisting—planning and relief work, for example.

In countries where private enterprise is not restricted, governments do not wish to compete with industry. Their unemployed do not manufacture goods for general consumption, but build dams, highways, stadiums, and recreation grounds. The production of armaments is also regarded as belonging to the same category of non-competitive activities. Arms can be produced in vast quantities without weakening the "armament market," since stored armaments affect that market about like "consumed" armaments.

In spite of the great influence of the armament industry, governments do hesitate less to nationalize or control the production of munitions because it is not very closely connected with market fluctuations. A great many books and articles keep people informed about the importance of the armament industry and the international links in it.

In the same way, people are learning more and more how the commercial power of trusts, cartels, and combines on the one hand is connected with the preparation for war on the other, since practically all production and trade are bound up with war. Profits and prices are connected with pain and death. Not a few people have been made conscious of the intense activities and complicated intrigues behind the scenes by novels and articles in periodicals dealing with such subjects.

Modern men learn to speak of nameless "money-powers" behind war-power. Once a specialty of radicals and a few university scholars, the theory of the commercial roots of war, the close connexion between war, commerce, and piracy, spreads throughout the world, and nobody knows exactly whether he is a "follower" of the theory or not. It is in the air.

Investments in foreign territories improve the commercial and financial and sometimes also the political position of investors, but in a great many cases they help a potential enemy.

When the press tells of the Pan-American road and transport system, of motor highways that join both the Americas from north to south, or of Imperial airways or other great international routes, it not only stresses the problems of travel, problems

82

of international contacts, but also the war interests which may be behind all.

In articles and books writers of different political and scientific faiths discuss possible combinations of war alliances, giving each an impressive name which may become the slogan of a future war. People are "Against Fascism," "Against the Comintern," "Against Aggressors," "For Democracy," "For Peace," "For Pacts," "For the League of Nations." Or they have the Pan-Asiatic idea, or the Pan-European, the Pan-German, the Pan-Turanian (a formula used during the World War to join the Magyars, Bulgars, and Turks as allies), the Pan-Slavic (a formula often heard before the World War), the Pan-American idea of the Monroe Doctrine. All these "pan" slogans are the daily bread of men. How quickly slogans and terms may die or change, directing the public "spontaneous enthusiasm" in the opposite direction, was to be seen at the beginning of the World War. As long as the Central Powers hoped to have Japan as their ally, they sometimes called the Japanese "the Prussians of the Far East." Later, when it became known that Japan was with the Allies, they called them "those yellow apes." One of the slogans which are now in the foreground: "Democracy fights Fascism," means Great Britain, France, the United States, and the Soviet Union are allied. If the Soviet Union is excluded, the "Western Democracies" remain. One can say the "Rome Pact" is revived, if Great Britain, France, Italy, and Germany co-operate, as by the Munich agreement for instance. The "French Pacts" which were nearly nullified on this occasion may be resurrected in a relatively short time. The connexions between Poland and the Soviet Union show how quickly international combinations can change. Some even see a possible rivalry between the United States and Great Britain and discuss the rivalry between Standard Oil and Royal Dutch-Shell. No alliance is impossible. History shows all kinds of alliances: a Cardinal as a French Prime Minister subsidizing the leader of the Protestants during the Thirty Years' War; the Christian King of France as the ally of the Turks against the Christian Hapsburgs.

If the whole political situation tends towards war, governments regroup themselves. War becomes imminent if the strength of both sides does not vary greatly. It may be assumed that countries of equal population have equal armies, that the governments have at their disposal the raw materials not only of their own territories but also of their dependencies and of countries with which they are closely connected, such as Great Britain and Canada. It is probable that in a future World War there will be fewer neutrals than in the last. In any case, it must be assumed that nearly all the world's resources of raw material will be at the disposal of the fighting countries. As a preliminary assumption, we may divide the resources of "other countries" into two.

Selecting certain raw materials which are of importance for armament and food, and taking as a basis the maximum of production in a country since 1929, we find the distribution of raw materials to be approximately the following for different alliances:

Silhouettes of War Economy

	Great Britain, France, Spain, Poland, Rumania, Hungary, Yugoslavia, Turkey, Iraq, Iran	United States, Soviet Union and other countries	Germany, Italy, Japan
Coal			
Petroleum			
Iron (content of ores)			
Copper (content of ores)			
Cotton and wool		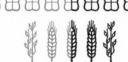	
Grain and rice			

	United States, Great Britain, France, Italy, Spain, Rumania, Hungary, Yugoslavia, Turkey, Iraq, Iran	Other countries	Soviet Union, Germany, Japan, Poland
Coal			
Petroleum			
Iron (content of ores)			
Copper (content of ores)			
Cotton and wool			
Grain and rice			

Each symbol represents 10 % of world production

84

Silhouettes of War Economy

**United States, Great Britain,
France, Soviet Union**

Other countries

**Germany, Italy, Japan, Spain,
Poland, Rumania, Hungary,
Yugoslavia, Turkey, Iraq, Iran**

Coal

Petroleum

**Iron
(content of ores)**

**Copper
(content of ores)**

Cotton and wool

Grain and rice

**United States, France,
Soviet Union, Turkey, Iraq, Iran**

Other countries

**Great Britain, Germany,
Italy, Japan, Spain, Poland,
Rumania, Hungary, Yugoslavia**

Coal

Petroleum

**Iron
(content of ores)**

**Copper
(content of ores)**

Cotton and wool

Grain and rice

Each symbol represents 10 % of world production

ISOTYPE

These schemes show only how the question of war can be discussed in concrete cases. Readers should not object that alliances are depicted which seem queer to them; a scheme is not a fact, and necessity makes strange bedfellows.

The study of such comprehensive groupings leads nearer to reality than the usual study of the "Big Seven" only. Certain alliances are interested in occupying neutral regions which provide certain raw materials. These are often more important than the raw materials and substitutes produced within the frontiers of the allies. Rubber and petroleum are among materials for which substitutes can be found only with difficulty.

To discuss the economics of war is not so unusual today as it was before the World War. Special economic measures necessary before and during a war are being foreseen and even taken. It is realized everywhere that during a war an expansion of planning is necessary.

Real planning is becoming universal—planning as a war measure, planning as an anti-depression medicine, and planning as the basis of a new social order. It may be said that planning is "fashionable," and, because it is widely imitated, also "modern," in spite of all theoretical criticism against a planned economy. In connexion with government relief work, plans have been much discussed and many suggested by labour parties. The chief aim nowadays is to fight world-wide unemployment, one of the most depressing conditions of our time. Unemployment insurance is a plaster to heal the wounds inflicted by the economic order. The elimination of unemployment is one of the striking features of the planned economy in the Soviet Union. This experience, but also special experience in other countries, in both democratic and authoritarian states, overcomes the objection that planning is too difficult and hence impossible.

New questions arise which have not yet been answered by historical experience. Can economic planning be combined with increasing civil liberty? What combinations of comprehensive social organization and free personal behaviour are possible? Will oppression be a transitory phenomenon or will it always be connected with planning, as a new social attitude?

Planning is not new. Only its widening scope and our becoming conscious of it are new. To a certain extent every primitive community, every agrarian community, every household, is based on planning. The primitives had no weapons to fight natural catastrophes; modern men have technical equipment to make life secure and to provide food and shelter, health and recreation for all. Every military organizer in history was a planner. Even today war economy in a great many countries is planned to a greater extent than peace economy. In the United States the seasonal fluctuations of coal-production accompanied by unemployment are permanent phenomena, in periods of prosperity and depression as well as in so-called normal years. Only during the World War was the seasonal fluctuation reduced to a minimum:

In War Seasonal Fluctuations Disappear
Quarterly Coal-Production in the United States

1914	1st	⛏⛏⛏⛏⛏⛏⛏⛏⛏ ⛏⛏
	2nd	⛏⛏⛏⛏⛏⛏⛏⛏
	3rd	⛏⛏⛏⛏⛏⛏⛏⛏⛏⛏ ⛏
	4th	⛏⛏⛏⛏⛏⛏⛏⛏⛏⛏ ⛏
1917	1st	⛏⛏⛏⛏⛏⛏⛏⛏⛏⛏ ⛏⛏⛏⛏
War	2nd	⛏⛏⛏⛏⛏⛏⛏⛏⛏⛏ ⛏⛏⛏⛏
	3rd	⛏⛏⛏⛏⛏⛏⛏⛏⛏⛏ ⛏⛏⛏⛏
	4th	⛏⛏⛏⛏⛏⛏⛏⛏⛏⛏ ⛏⛏⛏⛏
1922	1st	⛏⛏⛏⛏⛏⛏⛏⛏⛏⛏ ⛏⛏⛏
	2nd	⛏⛏⛏⛏⛏⛏
	3rd	⛏⛏⛏⛏⛏⛏⛏⛏⛏
	4th	⛏⛏⛏⛏⛏⛏⛏⛏⛏⛏ ⛏⛏⛏⛏
1926	1st	⛏⛏⛏⛏⛏⛏⛏⛏⛏⛏ ⛏⛏⛏⛏⛏
	2nd	⛏⛏⛏⛏⛏⛏⛏⛏⛏⛏ ⛏⛏
	3rd	⛏⛏⛏⛏⛏⛏⛏⛏⛏⛏ ⛏⛏⛏⛏
	4th	⛏⛏⛏⛏⛏⛏⛏⛏⛏⛏ ⛏⛏⛏⛏⛏⛏⛏
1932	1st	⛏⛏⛏⛏⛏⛏⛏⛏⛏
	2nd	⛏⛏⛏⛏⛏⛏
	3rd	⛏⛏⛏⛏⛏⛏⛏
	4th	⛏⛏⛏⛏⛏⛏⛏⛏⛏
1936	1st	⛏⛏⛏⛏⛏⛏⛏⛏⛏⛏ ⛏
	2nd	⛏⛏⛏⛏⛏⛏⛏⛏⛏
	3rd	⛏⛏⛏⛏⛏⛏⛏⛏
	4th	⛏⛏⛏⛏⛏⛏⛏⛏⛏⛏ ⛏⛏⛏

Each symbol represents 10 million short tons of coal, produced quarterly   ISOTYPE

Planning during war-time is so traditional that it need not be feared that mankind will require centuries of experience before a planned economy can be built up. The step from planned war economy to a planned peace economy has been taken with some degree of success by the Soviet Union. At present preparation for war often reduces unemployment and stimulates production. If a planned economy were a universal institution, the making of a good livelihood might then satisfy all important human needs, and war would become but a destroyer.

Some people doubt that war will ever disappear; they speak of the war "instinct." Some scientists, on the other hand, say that such an "instinct" does not exist. One historical fact serves to support such a thesis: in a region in which a great number of wars occurred during two hundred years, later there was hardly a war during another period of two hundred years:

Wars of Ancient Rome and Greece 400 B.C. to 200 B.C.

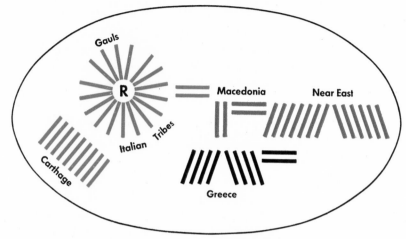

Each line represents 5 war years   red: Roman wars   black: Grecian wars before Philip and Alexander
blue: later wars in the region of Alexander's Empire

Wars of the Roman Empire 30 B.C. to 170 A.D.

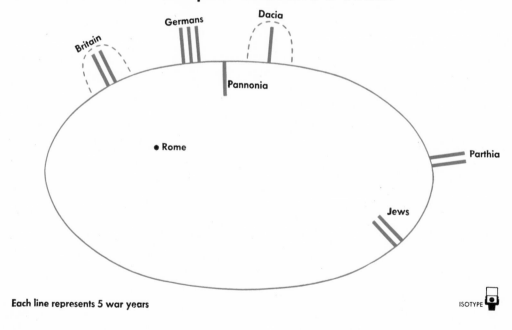

Each line represents 5 war years

ISOTYPE

88

Another chart might be added to demonstrate that in later centuries war was again frequent. The point is that the war situation may change rapidly. Though the fathers are accustomed to fighting, the sons may live in peace. Men are adapted to living in peace. War arises from certain circumstances. When they change, the desire or need to fight vanishes.

The idea that all human beings could live in peace within a comprehensive social framework spreads throughout the world in a period which is full of preparation for war and of internal disturbance. It is a characteristic of modern men and of the world situation that wars and economic depressions are no longer regarded as a matter of course, in spite of all the desire to use war as an instrument of profit, political power, or social change. An increasing opposition to war, a desire for peace and co-operation, characterizes the present social environment.

Like the "instinct" to fight, the "instinct" that opposes war is non-existent. People quickly learn different kinds of cruelty in peace-time. Nowadays it is the environment, the entanglement of various interests, that leads to war, and not a scarcity of food. There is no scarcity of food on the earth. Many more men might live on the products of the soil. There are also more efficient means to regulate the distribution of goods.

How to engineer a real world community is a problem which stimulates and irritates an increasing number of people. The pacifists are not the only ones who think that wars and internal disturbances constitute a burden like the Black Death. Many advocate only peace, others a new order as the basis of peace. One group thinks it is possible to fight these disasters only by means of weapons; another, that a kind of non-resistance, a general repudiation of all warlike behaviour should result in peace.

Militant Socialists combat pacifism for its own sake without glorifying war itself, while a great many militant nationalists glorify war and preach "heroism instead of pacifism." International tension is forcing an increasing number of governments to prepare for war. Even in states where opposition to the government is allowed, a great many people who object to war and fear every increase of militarization as a first step towards an authoritarian state nevertheless believe in military preparedness, because they fear—justifiably or unjustifiably—the victory of an authoritarian enemy and the expansion of totalitarianism by means of foreign armies more than the merely possible authoritarian effects of militarization.

The world situation is closely connected with the internal political and social situation of each country. To promote pacifism intensely is regarded more and more as a heresy not only in fundamentally militaristic states but also in the others as well. It is becoming very difficult to determine what the behaviour of the masses would be if the situation could be changed. Perhaps a certain flexibility is the result. A change in the social order which is not too violent and which is not connected with a change in men's character might lead to a most cruel period of war; another not too violent might lead to permanent peace. We may imagine human conflicts remaining as undirected as the particles in an unmagnetized bit of iron, or oriented by a magnetizing "war-machine."

This leads to the conclusion that international tension is based not on a real scarcity but on the structure of the human order of living. The conception of national planning is gaining ground in a world community which can hardly be called well organized. The factor "planning" is combined with changing political and social factors. The old order is entering into competition with planning, and the planning promoted by defence economy competes with non-planning and the kind of planning promoted by labour. Half planning promoted by ruling groups and their followers competes with complete planning; within a movement for total planned economy different groups may oppose one another. This world situation helps to form the social environment in which modern men grow up.

Social Environment

How different are the "silhouettes" of various nations! For good or evil, rich and poor states form the international background with its periods of prosperity and depression, with its production and destruction, with its war and peace. These rough contrasts do not present an adequate "profile of happiness" within a particular nation.

Conflicts between rich and poor create the social environment in which modern man grew up. They are sufficiently characterized by a "relief" showing different "strata" of incomes:

Profile of Personal Incomes in Great Britain, 1934

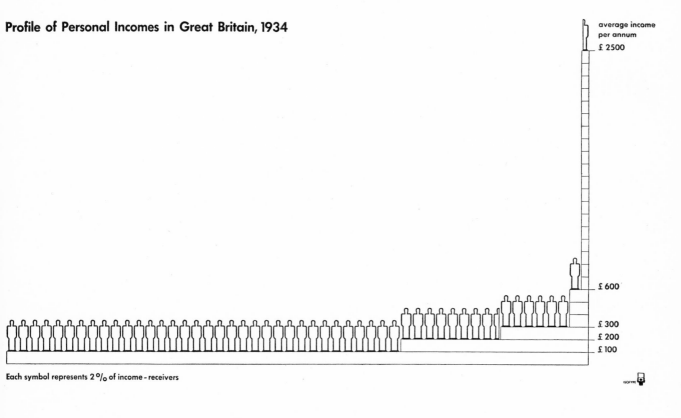

Each symbol represents 2 % of income - receivers

This "profile of happiness" shows enormous mountains and wide plains. No one now pleads that poverty is a necessary or worthy institution. A nation without paupers has no desire to create them. There are many causes of pauperism. It is in part a residue of the slavery of old:

Profile of Family Income in Columbia, South Carolina, 1933

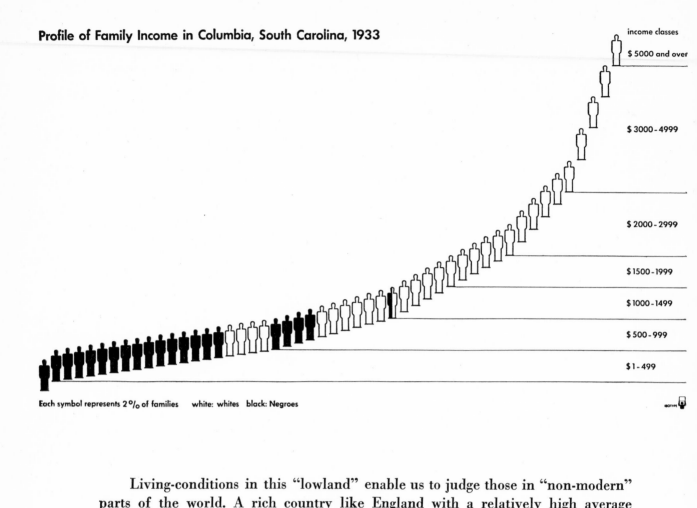

income classes

$ 5000 and over

$ 3000 - 4999

$ 2000 - 2999

$ 1500 - 1999

$ 1000 - 1499

$ 500 - 999

$ 1 - 499

Each symbol represents 2% of families   white: whites   black: Negroes

Living-conditions in this "lowland" enable us to judge those in "non-modern" parts of the world. A rich country like England with a relatively high average standard of living has many paupers in dreadful slums despite the high average income. The present housing movement started by clearing away slums, but not by clearing away pauperism as a whole. The distribution of large apartments, villas, beach houses on the one hand, of slums—"railroad flats" and crowded tenement houses in cities, and mud and log huts in the country—on the other, tells much about the distribution of human happiness. An increasing number of people realize that political problems of the present which are a characteristic of the social environment have no connexion with unknown or cosmic influences such as sun spots or with particular customs and opinions, but that they are a consequence of a social order which in spite of adequate natural resources does not allow full use of the real productive capacity and the complete elimination of pauperism.

Certain elements within the social pyramid seem to be more movable than others. Rich people can change their place of living easily; they can go where they like the climate, the surroundings, the social conditions, the low taxes. Those who travel first class find accommodations to their liking everywhere. First-class hotels and the villas of the Western rich are similar all over the world. As money can be invested everywhere, rich people are affected by distant events. Sometimes they even try to control the events by direct intervention or by appealing to their governments.

Another group which travels much is made up of the workers in manufacturing industries. Immigrants into the United States belong largely to this group of skilled or unskilled industrial workers, besides immigrants who are agricultural and domestic workers:

United States, Immigrants by Occupation

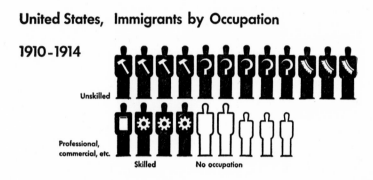

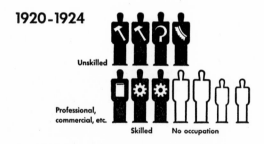

Each symbol represents 250,000 immigrants

Agricultural workers constitute another large group of immigrants—sons of peasant families with many children, seeking new sources of livelihood. And this despite the stability of the peasant group, which in many countries still is more stationary than are the city dwellers of today. The other groups, such as teachers, lawyers, physicians, belonging to the middle class, travel less and are more bound to their country. School diplomas and university degrees of one country are often not recognized in another. This handicaps migration. Men who have such certificates are interested in removing competitors, and not a few of them intend to develop stronger national ideas than other groups. As a rule it is this middle class that cultivates a taste for national folk-lore, old costumes, dances, games, and customs. This tendency is common to Western nations—the internationalism of nationalism.

95

There is another class which does not exist as a large group in all countries, but where it does exist is of a special type. This is the "fifth estate," the very poor, the hoboes, professional tramps, and gypsies, for whom there is no place in society. They must adapt themselves to the special irregularities in their social environment and make the most of the particular liberties which are left. Hence their character varies from place to place.

Social and hence living conditions vary widely in the United States, India, China, Great Britain, Japan, and the Soviet Union. Those who grow up in this environment must have very thick skins to bear a social situation in which the well-to-do live beside very poor people. Human character is not essentially altered by this juxtaposition; nor is life altogether unhappy. Though profits and also unemployment are eliminated in the Soviet Union by a new type of economic structure, there persist a middle-class level and a very low level. It follows that modernity is not over-sensitive about such distinctions—in the beginning.

It is difficult to study the budget of the poor. On the other hand a glance is enough to appraise human shelter.

Two Types of Tenements

Old Dumbbell Type covering 87% of the total area

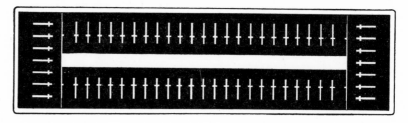

Modern Open Type covering 40% of the total area

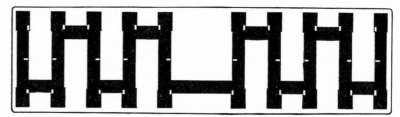

It is obvious that living-conditions are not without their influence on health. Disease is commoner among the poor than the prosperous. Abnormalities of body and mind occur more frequently in a poor environment. Badly fed bodies have less resistance, are feebler and smaller. Crude facts show this:

Living-Conditions and Mortality from Tuberculosis in Brooklyn
1929 - 1932

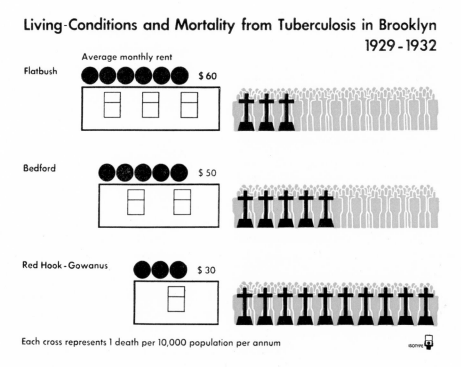

Each cross represents 1 death per 10,000 population per annum

In some countries the well-to-do are men with private income or aristocrats by birth, or both; in others they are, for example, members of a military or civil bureaucracy.

The ruling groups are connected in different ways. In industrialized countries men pass from official to commercial positions and vice versa. A high official in the foreign office may resign to become director of an industrial company or a bank. Bankers, promoters, entrepreneurs, contractors, and merchants are appointed financial and commercial advisers of governments and even government representatives abroad. They may be sent to organize protectorates in foreign territories or to act

97

as financial or military advisers to foreign states or native kings. A network of such appointments and their consequences covers the world. The friend of yesterday may become the spy of tomorrow; a general who advises a foreign government may the next moment be regarded as a traitor. All these actions and reactions depend upon decisions of ruling groups and cannot be regarded as following any scientific concept. Yet they play a significant part in the social environment. Conflicts between competing ruling groups and between the rich and the poor are important.

In the past, costume and dress indicated social standing and profession. In the Middle Ages Christians and Jews were distinguishable in the streets. In the Western countries, especially in countries like the United States or France, conformity to a single type of clothing may be a characteristic feature of modernization. Nevertheless even in these countries the well-to-do are separated from the poor not only by their better living-conditions but also by special customs, fashions, and whims introduced as barriers. Those excluded try to imitate people with an "air of good breeding."

In Continental Europe it was always possible to tell an artisan from a white-collar man, even when they were on holiday. In this region today party uniforms are of great importance. The militarization of the world stresses the difference between the military and the civilian population in most countries.

Differences between various groups of the population are maintained in many ways. In most countries, including the Soviet Union, different classes of railroad compartments or of accommodations on ships are found. These differentiations are not based on personal qualities; a poor man has the right to buy a ticket for a Pullman car. But other differentiations discriminate between persons. There are different compartments for coloured and white people on the trains in Indo-China and in the South of the United States; separate benches are reserved for Jews and non-Jews in public parks of Germany, where, as in other central European countries, new discriminating laws have been issued. That type of discrimination which is independent of one's financial standing does not seem to be a component of modernity, and is not deeply rooted in the countries into which it has been introduced recently.

A greater facility in changing from one social group to another does, however, characterize modernity. But it is difficult completely to eliminate the many differentiations between classes imposed by upbringing, education, and environment. Many people, therefore, remain in the social group in which they were born, and follow an occupation similar to that of their parents. Thus they are bound to a special type of life: to certain dangers connected with their occupation, to the prevalence of disease in their environment, to the way of living and mode of recreation of their associates. Most marriages are between persons of the same social standing, and so are most friendships.

The present social environment is charged with tendencies to change the conditions of living. Some of these threaten the social order itself. Scientific hypotheses that purport to indicate the transformation of social orders can be made and the main forces in the field sought, but how can the relation between conscious action and the level of human happiness be visualized? Facts are the resultants of various forces. There is no doubt, for instance, that strikes express one type of dissatisfaction, but it cannot be said that an increasing number of strikes necessarily indicates an increasing dissatisfaction among workers.

Steel-Production in United States

1927
1928
1929
1930
1931
1932
1933
1934
1935
1936

Each symbol represents 5 million long tons

Strikes in United States

Each symbol represents
5 million days lost

ISOTYPE

99

Strikes are called generally when the chance of success is good—that is, in periods of incipient prosperity. Workers will also seize opportunities to entrench themselves when their security is threatened. Despite the restlessness that followed the collapse of 1929 they do not usually strike during economic depressions. In totalitarian countries, where strikes are forbidden, it is difficult to detect evidences of proletarian discontent though it may be seething below the surface.

The vote cast for policies and candidates for office, articles in newspapers, and similar forms of expression give an unsatisfactory picture of attitudes in a certain environment. In countries where there is no freedom of speech and of the press, "public opinion" cannot be deduced from newspaper articles; even in countries in which newspapers are free to print what they like, there is no close correlation between articles and public opinion.

Public Opinion

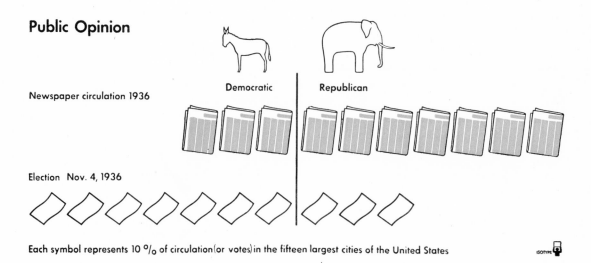

Newspaper circulation 1936

Democratic   Republican

Election Nov. 4, 1936

Each symbol represents 10 % of circulation(or votes) in the fifteen largest cities of the United States

The present age has created certain institutions which make it possible for dissatisfaction to be expressed freely. The election of representatives to a parliament, the formation of parties, and political activity, which have been part of the governmental system of some states in the last few centuries, depend upon freedom of opposing forces. Some groups hope that by changing the balance of these forces the whole social order may slowly be changed, and some think that poverty and insecurity may be finally eliminated by such means. Other groups advocate a one-party system, either because they fear that certain changes to which they object may otherwise be made or because they think that important reforms which they desire cannot be effected in the face of opposition.

100

Political Organization

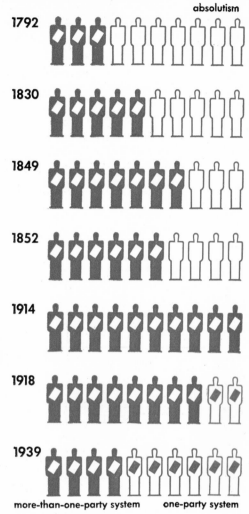

1792

absolutism

1830

1849

1852

1914

1918

1939

more-than-one-party system   one-party system

Each symbol represents
10% of the population of America, Europe, and the Soviet Union

Blue: people living under a "profit" system
    without ballot paper: no suffrage
    with white ballot paper: non-authoritarian states
    with blue ballot paper: authoritarian states
Red: people living under a "non-profit" system (the Soviet Union)

After 1792 absolutism, with its feudal elements, vanished and constitutionalism spread. The "political conflagration" of the French Revolution has not been repeated in all countries. In some, relatively minor disturbances ended by changing the social and political order. In many, the ruling groups, while adopting some elements of constitutionalism, tried to preserve some of their power within the new order. Families of feudal origin, for instance, tried to become owners of factories and to secure for their offspring good government positions or commissions in the armies and navies of newly industrialized and commercialized states. Each world-wide social transformation moves in a complicated path. The industrialized Britons, for instance, supported the forces of tradition in Europe by supporting the alliance against Napoleonic France, which adopted British policies and thus came into competition with Great Britain. It would not have been difficult for Britons to have allied themselves with Napoleon under some such formula as "against the reactionary states," after having approved the French Revolution.

It is difficult to predict how changes in society will come about, if imitations of other countries' institutions and possible alliances are borne in mind. The social environment may be characterized by three qualities:

Chessboard of Social Qualities

	More-than-one-party system	Profit system	International Labour Contacts
Great Britain	yes	yes	yes
France	yes	yes	yes
Italy	no	yes	no
Germany	no	yes	no
Soviet Union	no	no	yes

Though states may be bound by tradition, it may also happen that, as the result of a wave of planning, new political structures arise out of the old. Thus the ruling classes of an authoritarian structure may resort to planning to consolidate their privileges. Or a multi-party system may combine planning with the preservation of privileges. Or privileges may be abolished and planning attuned to a multi-party system. At present an economy of national defence compels governments to prepare for the expected next world war.

In view of this the alliances of the near or more distant future cannot be predicted. Co-operation between France and the Soviet Union might be based on the anti-Fascism of the People's Front, but that could scarcely be the basis for co-operation between Great Britain, France, Italy, and the Soviet Union. If Germany wished to join the Soviet Union against a common enemy, the Comintern would have to be at least tacitly accepted or condoned.

All such alliances influence the transformation of the economic order and the total social environment. This influence is perhaps relatively weak, and the historical trend of the social environment could be described without mentioning all the daily fluctuations in the relations between governments. Instead, the trend might be inferred from the signs of incipient international co-operation and unification.

It is increasingly recognized that the abolition of poverty, unemployment, war, and racial discrimination, all more or less interdependent, is closely connected with the agencies that are modifying the present social order. But other organized efforts may profoundly affect life without seriously changing the social order, as, for example, the fight against catastrophes such as floods and drought, which is similar to the fight against epidemics, and the restoration of the damage done by tornadoes and earthquakes.

These well-planned activities present many features of modernity. Moreover they have a long tradition behind them. The civilization in the valleys of the Euphrates and the Tigris, the Egyptian and the Chinese civilizations were all based on agricultural co-operation, which was an essential part of the social order.

Irrigation is important today in certain countries—for instance, in Egypt, China, India, Italy, Spain, Mexico, and in parts of the United States and the Soviet Union.

Fields are often irrigated by states which are building dams and dikes, as in the Netherlands, where new land has been made by holding back the sea. The population of the temperate zones, where there is sufficient rain, has learned relatively late to organize irrigation and to control rivers co-operatively. Oriental nations seem to have been the teachers of Western peoples not only in irrigation and flood-control, but also in intensive agriculture as a whole.

Technical evolution has reached such a high level that all flood catastrophes can be fought successfully by known technical methods. In the United States, for instance, gigantic dams are built, which not only tend to control floods but assure a water-supply for various purposes, such as the irrigation of land and the generation of electric energy.

Since comprehensive flood-control leads to government control of energy through reforestation, the prevention of erosion, and other important conservation measures, there is much discussion of possible social changes that such federal intervention might bring about. Some fear a restriction of trade and profits, whether through the elimination of competitors by ruling groups, who in this way might secure large permanent incomes for their families, or through Fascism or Socialism spread by governmental institutions among the masses by improving their living-conditions. Some hold that centralization might result in suppression of freedom of the press and of speech; others that technical control is possible with a large amount of personal freedom: in other words, control of production without control of thinking.

It may be seen at a glance that the control of the basin of the Mississippi River alone needs the co-operation of over twenty states. The area of this basin is over a third that of the United States:

The Basin of the Mississippi and Its Tributaries

ISOTYPE

This is not the place to analyse the reason why people did not build their shelters far from river banks that may be flooded. Problems of trade and transportation influenced their decision. Great floods are a characteristic of the social environment of many countries—for instance, of China and the United States. In certain states, such as Louisiana, about fifteen per cent of the population was afflicted by the great flood of 1927:

The Flooded Area near the Estuary of the Mississippi and Its Population

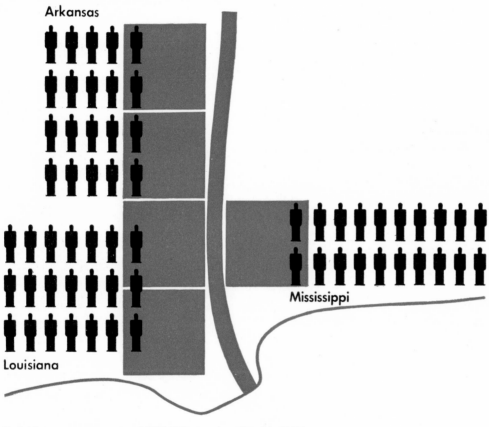

Each blue square represents 2,500,000 acres inundated in 1927
Each man symbol represents 100,000 population of states
on blue: population of flooded area

In China tremendous devastation is caused by floods, and the country lacks the well-organized relief which is a characteristic of the United States.

The main efforts to control floods are inseparable from efforts to organize irrigation. The civilization of the present time does not so much depend upon irrigation as, for example, ancient Egypt did. In our times, too, irrigation is essential in Egypt. In Egypt irrigation is more widespread than in Mexico, and in Mexico more than in the United States:

Area Irrigated

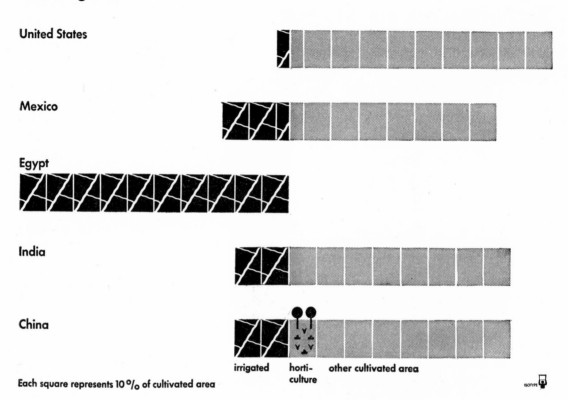

United States

Mexico

Egypt

India

China

irrigated   horti-   other cultivated area
             culture

Each square represents 10 % of cultivated area

Irrigation seems to be more important at present because the exhaustion of the soil, as the result of unscientific cultivation, forces men on the one hand to combat erosion and expand irrigation, and on the other to produce more, as is necessary, for instance, in Mexico.

Flood-control and extension of irrigation lead to certain types of continual co-operation. Earthquakes and tornadoes come and go, and cannot be predicted. Scientists know only that certain regions are more exposed to them than others. Earthquakes and tornadoes cannot be regulated. On the other hand, shelters and other buildings which have been wrecked by them can be rebuilt. Such organized reconstruction is similar to the reconstruction that followed the World War in France and Belgium. The success of these enterprises is based on the fact that in the social order of today a great many reserves can be drawn upon which exist in spite of what we may call "the permanent economic depression," for prosperity may be regarded as a

Maximum Stocks since 1930
Compared with Annual Production

Wheat 1934

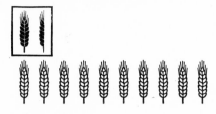

Sugar 1932

Coffee 1931/33

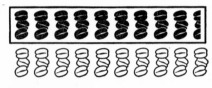

Cotton 1932/33

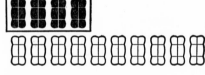

Rubber 1935

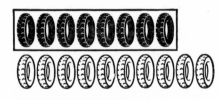

Petroleum 1930

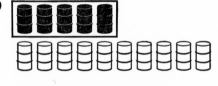

Copper 1932

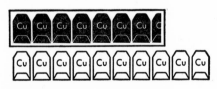

Each symbol represents 10% of annual production

white symbols: produced annually
black symbol in rectangles: still in stock from previous years

"lesser depression" since productive capacity is always higher than actual production.

Huge world stocks of food and raw materials have been accumulated by society today. They will help to rebuild a world which may suffer the destruction wrought by war or an earthquake. But in the world of the future, reconstruction after disaster would not bring about a quasi-prosperity, as it does now, since reserves for emergencies will be more carefully planned.

Co-operation on a large scale marks social environment today. Men learn the necessity for co-operation and planning in different fields of social life. It is apparent on every hand that famine and poverty cannot be attributed to lack of resources. Highly efficient means of communication, some developed during the World War, have overcome barriers that once separated countries.

Fairly rapid communication was always possible. In the ancient Roman Republic only citizens actually in Rome could influence politics by electing representatives. Nobody ever thought of sending to Rome representatives elected by Romans in Alexandria or Massilia. In the Middle Ages popes were elected by the people of Rome and then by cardinals who travelled to Rome to cast their votes. Even today if a cardinal is ill or prevented by war or otherwise from going to Rome to vote, he may not send a deputy. Nor may a member of Parliament vote by proxy if he is ill, and this though the absence of powerful spokesmen through illness might mean the defeat of important measures. Television, coupled with the radio or wire telephone, makes it possible to "attend" a parliamentary meeting by electricity and thus to overcome the handicap of distance or physical disability. It is possible to imagine a parliamentary debate carried on by widely separated representatives who may even make themselves so objectionable by shouts and gestures that the chairman is obliged to switch them off. The increase in the use of the telephone, radio, the automobile, and other means of communication can prepare the way for a virtually international co-operation of humanity.

Radio, Telephone, Automobiles

Each symbol represents 1 million radios, telephones, automobiles

Curiously enough, the technological improvement of communication is at present attended by a restriction of freedom of speech in some countries. Possibly the restriction may ultimately be removed so that radio broadcasting and other means of mass appeal and rapid communication will be permitted to perform their proper function of making nations better acquainted with one another.

Only a part of the world is involved in this process of technological change, and this part alone may be regarded as the place of origin of modern mechanized civilization. It may be assumed that all land fifty miles to the right and left of a railroad has the potentiality of mechanized modernity.

Communities thus favourably located are able to fight flood, famine, and other disasters. Foodstuffs are stocked not for the happiness of men, but for profit. Nevertheless they make it possible to cope with famine if it occurs.

The expanding of the international railroad system is closely connected with the expanding of the basis of modern life, as one might see from the modern history of both the Americas:

Territory within 50 Miles of a Railroad

1863

1913

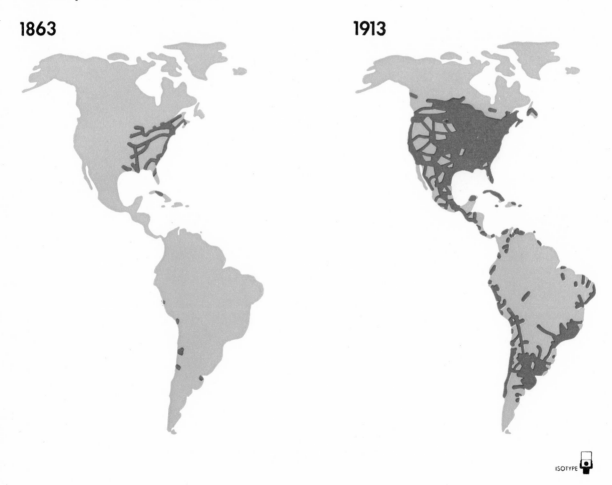

ISOTYPE

Scientists learn more and more how to change the surface of the earth, how to create new seas in central Africa or to overcome the disadvantages of an unfavourable climate. Even Iceland's geysers supply warm water to heat houses. But men have not learned to predict or stop earthquakes or to prevent volcanoes from erupting. Such possibilities of science are not so important at the moment as abolishing the possibility of war, unemployment, and oppression, which are the great blots on our time and, together with the "profit system," the main characteristics of the present social environment.

Man's Daily Life

What do all these trends towards modernity mean in man's daily life? What changes have taken place in each individual life? How can the social facts be retold in terms of individual experience?

One actual change in personal life is traceable to the fact that the birth-rate is decreasing. Modern children grow up in relatively small families. The "only child," an exception in the past, is becoming more and more the rule. When there are more children in a family, often several years lie between their births. If a boy has a sister who is his junior by six years, each grows up practically as an "only child," with all the peculiarities that characterize this situation. In an old-fashioned family there were many brothers and sisters, uncles and aunts, cousins, and other relatives; today many children have no uncles.

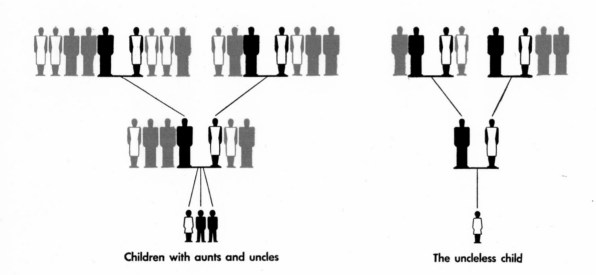

Children with aunts and uncles   The uncleless child

A child knows that it has parents and that nearly all of the other people of its acquaintance are not relatives. The "only child" is an urgent modern social problem, which, as a special subject of research, is being discussed by psychologists, pedagogues and physicians. A child needs not only playmates but also close relatives.

Children of 3 to 5 Years of Age in the Netherlands

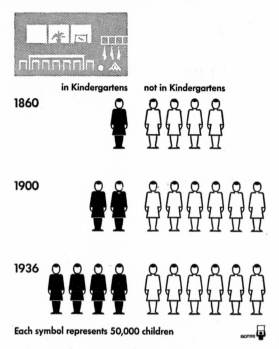

	in Kindergartens	not in Kindergartens
1860		
1900		
1936		

Each symbol represents 50,000 children

The "only child" does not easily learn within the family how to adapt itself to its environment. Hence kindergartens are necessary not only for modern pedagogy in general, but also for mental hygiene. Large families in the past constituted collective educational groups. Today a decrease in the birth-rate forces parents to support all kinds of children's communities. An increase in the number of kindergartens, playgrounds, and other institutions intended for children parallels the decrease in the number of children in families. Education in children's communities is the first step in adapting the human being to social life.

This collectivization of the life of children is connected not only with the trend in the birth-rate but also with other changes. More mothers than before work in factories and offices and are glad to have their children kept off the street and away from its dangers. Formerly women worked more at home. The peasant's wife and daughters always worked with him, as did the female members of the artisan's family. The middle-class household at the beginning of the nineteenth century was a very extensive organization, with baking and slaughtering and sewing carried on at home. Within such a household the women had much responsible work. When the industrial revolution introduced machinery for sewing, baking, and slaughtering, women were left without any really technical responsibility. Many middle-class women then began to direct their interest towards fields outside their families. They took an active part in social life.

114

The expansion of woman suffrage in the twentieth century is connected with these changes.

Political Rights of Women

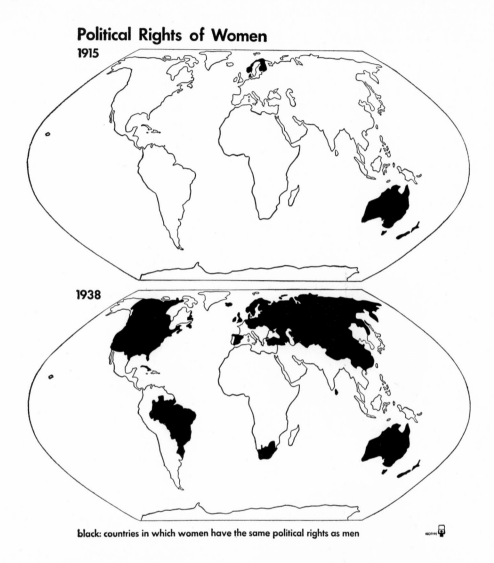

1915

1938

black: countries in which women have the same political rights as men

In more countries than ever before women are now admitted to universities and to learned professions. Women artists, writers, orators, physicians, teachers, private and public officials are no longer uncommon. How modernization is accompanied by the emancipation of women is especially noticeable in the eastern republics of the Soviet Union, and also in Turkey, Persia, and other Asiatic countries into which modernization has penetrated. Veils are vanishing; so is the segregation of men and women. Even in backward communities women learn to read and write, and take part in social and political life.

The workman's wife and children were forced to go into the factory when they could no longer help their husband or father at home. Wages of the man alone could not provide for the whole family. Family life could not flourish. Children were a burden in the early period of industrialization; they were made to work when very young, to increase the family income. Many children were an economic blessing, thus considered. Hence younger children were often better fed than the first born, as a matter of financial expediency.

All this has greatly changed with the mechanization of factory processes, the reduction of working hours, and the better wages brought about by strikes and the growing political influence of the working classes, or with the need of armies composed of well-fed, healthy fighters rather than of half-starved wretches.

Work, Leisure, Sleep

Formerly

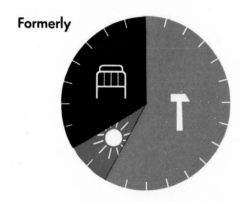

Now

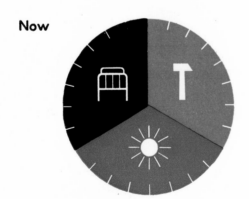

Subdivision of the 24 hours of a day
red: work   blue: leisure   black: sleep

However motivated, social welfare cannot ward off unemployment, which plunges part of the population back into poverty, often destroys family life, and forces workers to take to the road in caravans or on foot as hoboes. This "fifth estate" constitutes part of the population of every glamorous metropolis.

During the World War many women had to take men's places. After the war they were forced out of industries before the men. In both Fascist and non-Fascist countries it was trumpeted that "woman's place is in the family and the home." Now that hands are needed in the preparation for war, the slogan has changed to: "Woman must be regarded as man's helpmate." This is another step towards the equalization of men and women, and hence towards modernization of the relation of men and women. The wives of unemployed men often try to earn some money by working. This means that the husband has to do the housework and care for the children. The conception of a wife as a cheap servant is vanishing. Though we are still living in a "male society," the expansion of the rights of women and girls is a characteristic of modernity. And the exercise of these rights is no longer restricted to the office or the home.

Once only the males of a community had the privilege of indulging in sports. Nowadays men and women may actually compete in gymnastics or in athletics. Even in Germany, where every girl is regarded as a potential housewife and mother, the old distinction has broken down, and girls and boys are trained in the open by common instructors.

Sports are an element of modern life; huge crowds watch a football game:

Football at American Colleges

1920

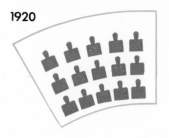

1930

Each section represents seating facilities for 1 million spectators
Each man symbol represents 100,000 spectators

117

The youth not only of the well-to-do but also of the lower classes engage in athletic sports such as swimming, walking, or football and join athletic clubs or teams if their bodies are not too exhausted by work or poverty. This interest in sports is developing to such a degree that it must be regarded as a manifestation of modernity.

This evolution of athletic sports is closely connected with preparations for war. Even the Olympic games can also be regarded as a factor in the comprehensive militarization of public institutions and private life. Becoming or keeping fit through exercise is accepted on principle in Great Britain, the Soviet Union, Germany, and the United States. Exercise is often connected with "hikes" or marches or with instruction and practice in first aid. Mere boys know how to use the rifle in Italy and other countries. In Switzerland this is an old tradition. Military training is provided in certain American universities. Physical exercise enhances the military power of a nation even if it is not directly connected with military drilling and training. English clerks well trained in sports became good soldiers in the World War. In many countries among the younger generation of the upper classes we find civilian aviation clubs and similar organizations, most of which have, directly or indirectly, the idea of national defence behind them. Ours is an atmosphere of war. In Great Britain, a non-militaristic nation, a new Territorial Army badge has been introduced, which may be worn by all ranks when in mufti, symbolizing service in the Territorial Army. The first immigrants into New England also lived in such a warlike atmosphere. Pictures showing men carrying muskets on their way to church with their families are familiar. Fighting was endemic in that day. Today war is like an epidemic, breaking out from time to time. Military equipment for killing human beings is regarded as necessary to state organization; parades of soldiers are spectacles. Uniforms and flirtation, military bands and celebrations are closely connected in Western civilization. Armies are the embodiment of businesslike practice on the one hand (through the progressive elimination from soldiers' drill of all superfluous movements in certain countries), and on the other hand the colourful and resounding representatives of governments, parties, and other institutions. The introduction into the Italian army of the "Roman step," which is a variation of the Prussian "goose-step," is an example of the unification of militarization. The militarization of public and private life has placed a premium on youth.

Athletic sports and militarism are powerful influences. Saluting, flag-signalling or wigwagging, and similar demonstrations, adapted to the customs of different countries, are common in public life. The collectivization of modern life is prepared for by this development, while simultaneously the youth of both sexes is freed from the paternal tradition. The right of youth to a personal life of its own within the family, with freedom for study or devotion to arts or science, is acknowledged. The principle that a girl or a boy needs his own room and should not be forced to live always among adults is generally applied where the standard of living allows it. The declining birth-rate facilitates this. Boys and girls still live in different worlds, but the differences are not as sharp as they once were. In all classes leisure, recreation, education, are essential. One remarkable difference, however, remains unchanged. The childhood of girls and boys of the working classes ends at about the age of fourteen; young men and women of more than fifteen go to work as adults. The boys and the girls of the upper classes, on the other hand, enjoy a few more years of childhood, years which are filled with study, exercise, and recreation.

Recreation and education are more common today than they were a hundred years ago. The masses achieved these privileges partly as concessions from above after organized protests and political struggle, and occasionally as the result of a revolution, as in the Soviet Union. There is more and more leisure, whatever various religious, political, and other attitudes may be. Evidently modern man intends to organize work and recreation. International commercial competition has equalized this trend in all countries represented in the world market. A mill hand whose working conditions in Manchester are better than those of his fellow in India is haunted by the fear that his British employer may be forced to increase working hours. British manufacturers fear the competition of cheap labour. Hence, their direct interest in labour regulations abroad when they find it impossible to augment working hours at home. General reduction of working hours may occur with increasing unemployment. Workers and employers are both influenced by these forces. Working hours can be reduced by the usual type of international agreement, but not unemployment, which requires a higher type of organized effort. A large proportion of the labouring class is demanding more leisure and better living-conditions. Another group is in rebellion against the present social order as a whole. Reduction of working time is a positive achievement. It means more time for recreation, more happiness.

One requirement has remained constant throughout the centuries: the amount of sleep man needs. To reduce that is to undermine his health. And since it varies little, long working hours mean in general less leisure. The general trend towards more leisure means a profound change in daily life, not only for the masses, but also for ruling groups. On the European continent, for instance, during the nineteenth century high officials were not given free Sundays. A free week-end means a reorganization of private life.

With more leisure and more spare money a new family life is possible. The home has new attraction to minds and bodies not exhausted by overwork.

Technological advance has contributed much towards making the home more attractive. Washing-machines, vacuum cleaners, sewing-machines, gas stoves and oil furnaces that do away with shovelling coal, push-button conveniences, radio sets, phonographs, and motion-picture projectors have made the home more than merely a place where weary workers may snatch a few hours' needed sleep.

Modern Devices in Different Income Classes

Columbia, South Carolina

$ 1-499

$ 1500-1999

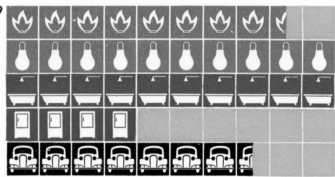

$ 7000 and over

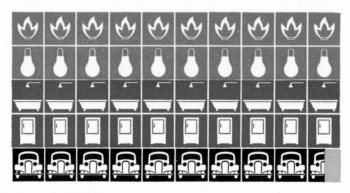

The number of homes out of 10 which have:

Gas for cooking   Electric light   Bathtubs or showers   Refrigerators   Automobiles   ISOTYPE

Family life in the city is different from family life on the farm. By tradition a farmer rises at dawn (even before dawn in winter) and toils until sundown, with a rest at noon for the principal meal of the day. When night falls he is at home. He goes to bed not much later than barnyard fowls go to roost. Working hours are determined by the length of the day and by the season. With urbanization and the electrification of the home there comes independence of the sun. Night is more than the time for sleep. This becomes apparent when we consider the hours when city folk and farmers take their meals.

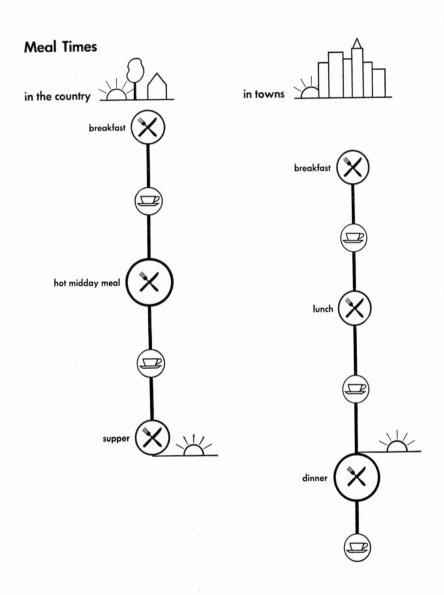

Meal Times

in the country

breakfast

hot midday meal

supper

in towns

breakfast

lunch

dinner

Dinner no longer marks an interval between periods of work. Leisure, prolonged into a night which is an artificial day, is spent partly at home, partly in cinemas, public libraries, and theatres and partly at sports and games. There is now more interest in pure fun than in drinking, which once occupied the short leisure of old. The shortening of the working day has changed life more than have all the inventions which have made it possible to organize leisure on a broad scale.

Seating Accommodation in Theatres, Music Halls and Cinemas in the County of London, per 100 population

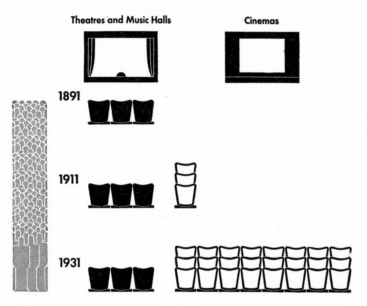

Each single black symbol represents 1 seat per 100 population in theatres and music halls
Each set of three white symbols represents 1 seat per 100 population in cinemas
(on an average 3 performances daily)

The invention of radio made indoor life more attractive and gave a new meaning to the hearth after the rush and unrest of the day. People are not "set" in their ways or "dyed in the wool." They have within themselves resources that await development. When one special part of man's character is brought out, some opposite is brought out too. It is not true that the "mechanization" of work breeds a love for more mechanization. It is possible to turn an oil valve and thus to flood a house with heat. Yet, despite the oil furnace in the cellar, we often find logs crackling in a fireplace and reviving memories of what we call "the good old times" of our grandfathers. Life in homes with first-class plumbing does not stifle a desire for camping, hunting, or "hiking."

The automobile, which is a part of the usual equipment of Americans, together with other means of transportation, has brought about another important change in man's daily life. Men can now travel farther than formerly in the same space of time. As a consequence of this, towns are expanding even faster than their populations are growing. Home and place of work are often very far apart. In other words, though the distance from home to work is much longer, the time necessary to cover it has not changed much. Many people who have to work in the unrest of the city like a quiet home. The population of the business centre is decreasing everywhere in favour of suburbs.

In spite of the industrial revolution ushered in by the steam engine, the rhythm of personal life did not always change. In a great many respects, however, modern technology opens new prospects for a greater number of people. A rich man in ancient Rome could obtain light instantly if he wished. He would clap his hands and a dozen servants would bring torches and lamps. Nowadays anybody who has electric light in his home can always obtain light instantly. Such conveniences are more widely used than formerly, and there are many more which have yet to be put to general use.

Inventions that speed up travel have not radically changed modern man's general sense of relative proximity to the farthest outposts of the civilized world. The Roman Empire, for instance, comprised about all the regions with which the ancients were directly concerned.

London
The Population Moves to the Suburbs

1851

1891

1935

Each symbol represents 100,000 population
Innermost circle: City, Finsbury, Holborn
Second circle: County of London
Outer circle: Greater London

123

The time it takes to travel with heavy luggage from New York to Singapore—about three weeks—is approximately the same as the time it took to travel from Spain to Asia Minor.

The longest distance between two points on the earth's surface is an arc of 180°. From Spain to Asia Minor is about 36°.

Travelling Distances in the Ancient Roman Empire

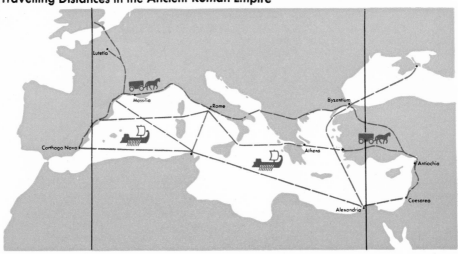

Each unit of distance represents one travelling day   red: on land   blue: on sea   ISOTYPE

Travelling Distances Nowadays

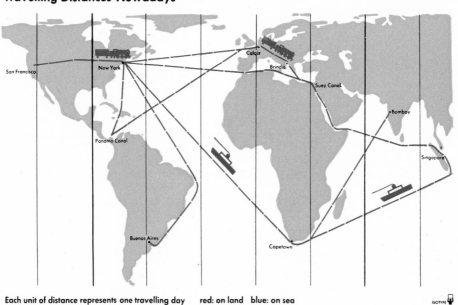

Each unit of distance represents one travelling day   red: on land   blue: on sea   ISOTYPE

124

Much more than by technical development, personal life has been changed by the prolongation of life, by the reduction of the death-rate. A modern child does not learn what death means as early as did a child of past times. It does not often happen now that parents, brothers, sisters, or playmates die during the formative years of a child. In Western countries parents were formerly more accustomed to losing children by death, as they are now in countries where the public health service is badly organized.

Though accidents are not the principal cause of death, they occupy an important place in mortality tables, not only because they occur to people in the best of health, but also because, as everybody knows, they may be largely avoided by better safety measures. Especially industrial accidents, which are more or less expected and taken into account by management, give rise to protest. It is often pointed out that the human lives sacrificed by mismanagement of work or inadequate protection outnumber the deaths due to war—in other words, the mismanagement of world society.

The number of cases of tuberculosis can be largely reduced. American and other experience demonstrates that the toll that it exacts can be reduced to the same extent as death from accidents. Again the responsibility must be laid at the door of social mismanagement. That the plague and cholera vanished from the modern world, that the incidence of typhoid fever, tuberculosis, and many other diseases has been largely reduced, means that a man born today under more

Infant Mortality. Tuberculosis. Accidents.

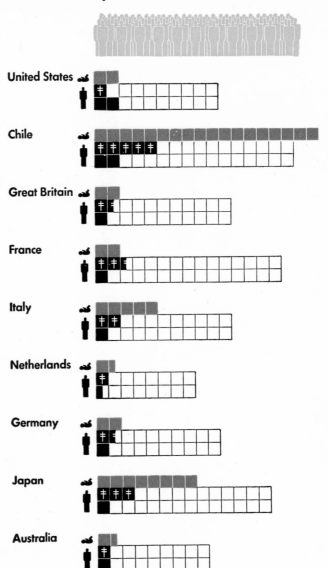

Each square represents 5 deaths per 10,000 population, annually

first row: infant death-rate
second and third row: death-rate above the age of 1
with double cross: from tuberculosis   black: from external causes
outline: others   (accidents, homicide)

125

or less the same circumstances as were his ancestors may be expected to reach a greater age than if he had been born a century ago. But if he lives beyond childhood, his chance of reaching old age is not much better than was that of his great-grandfather. This can be seen from a comparison of average ages at death now and formerly. The gain has been made in reducing infant mortality.

The rapid decline in the death-rate causes war deaths to stand out glaringly. If the number of those who die on the battlefield or from wounds received in battle remains constant, war will be more than ever like a terrible epidemic. During and after the Middle Ages deaths caused by the plague were so high that deaths which were the result of war seemed low in comparison.

Large families in the past were repeatedly forced to put on mourning for relatives and friends. They were familiar with the rites associated with death and burial and therefore with churches and congregations too. Even less religiously inclined people came into contact with their clergymen in connexion with birth, marriage, and death. How can one test the state of religion? Is the Church losing or gaining ground as society changes?

Silhouette of a Town

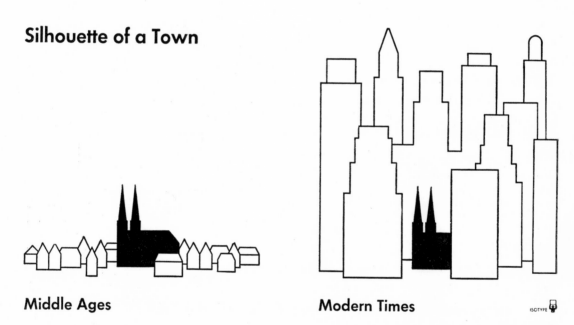

Middle Ages   **Modern Times**

In the Middle Ages each church was built for a certain number of persons. The size of a community could be judged by the size of the church. As a rule the church was also the biggest building in a town. This is no longer true. There are many more adults in a town nowadays than there are seats in the churches.

Modern men are freer than were their forebears from church ties. This does not mean that they are free from all connexion with the Church. Many do not put

126

the teachings of their churches into practice. It is difficult to make an international survey of these changes. This increasing freedom is connected on the one hand with an increasing understanding of how to influence other people by words, and on the other with certain kinds of training in behaviour and thinking. The idea that a priest's wise words could be a substitute for medicine has been discarded. More and more men understand the power of words. The importance of personal training is more appreciated in the Western world, as it has long been appreciated in Asia. The Catholic Church, no longer internationally predominant, is now only one church among others.

How can the influence of churches on individuals be measured? The increase of suicide is one test. It indicates a decreasing ecclesiastical influence in certain regions. The growing practice of birth-control is another sign. Though contrary to the teachings of most Christian churches, birth-control is now widespread. In some countries the Church is still strong enough to oppose the practice successfully. On this point statistics are more informative than speeches and pamphlets. The evidence shows that birth-control started in the higher social classes. As far back as 1900 it was beginning to gain ground:

Births per 100 Married Women, between 15 and 50 Years of Age about 1900

in Paris

Poor districts

Intermediate districts

Rich districts

in Vienna

Poor districts

Intermediate districts

Rich districts

In many countries representatives of the ruling classes passed laws punishing promotion of birth-control though they themselves practised it; but they also knew how to escape the legal difficulties which might arise as the result of their practices. After a period of advocating birth-control, the government of the Soviet Union prohibited abortion and brought forward certain objections to birth-control. Hence at the moment birth-control is under scrutiny all over the world. Since there are difficulties in producing food and building homes for the population, most governments, while prohibiting instruction in methods of birth-control, try to justify their demands for an increase in population partly by promoting moral and religious ideas, partly by stressing the doctrine that a strong nation needs military power.

The amount of premarital sexual intercourse in all classes of the Western countries is increasing because birth-control protects a woman's good name particularly in countries where giving birth to an illegitimate child is a disgrace. Many young girls no longer feel bound by parental admonition in these matters. They lead their own lives, especially if they support themselves, arrive at judgments by themselves, especially if family ties have been broken. Premarital intercourse is common in certain rural districts. Hence urban and rural morals are now much the same. This is not a sign of urban "decadence." In certain regions where birth-control is unusual, widespread premarital sexual intercourse can be proved by means of the high percentage of illegitimate births.

The predominant influence of the Catholic Church seems to prevent birth-control in Austria, but not, to the same extent, premarital sex connexions, which are traditional. In other countries the situation is very different. The Mohammedan tradition prevents premarital sex connexions and illegitimate births in Algeria.

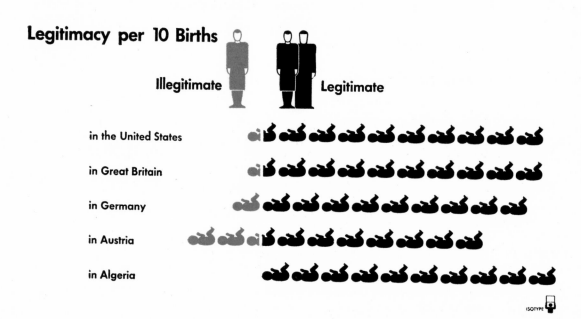

Legitimacy per 10 Births

Illegitimate   Legitimate

in the United States

in Great Britain

in Germany

in Austria

in Algeria

ISOTYPE

128

It may be assumed that a great many love problems that might have ended disastrously are solved in modern times, because, according to statistics, unrequited love is no longer so decisive a factor in suicide as formerly. Young people encounter fewer difficulties in finding their mates than before. Celibacy among young men is rare, even in the middle classes. The boundaries between the different ages seem to have been removed. Not only the length of life, but also youth has been prolonged, with health and love. But conflicts and fear based on social difficulties haunt the youth of today as much as adults. The fluidity of business and the world situation has its effect on the social environment, and hence on daily life. A chart symbolizes this personal situation at the end of a "bad" year:

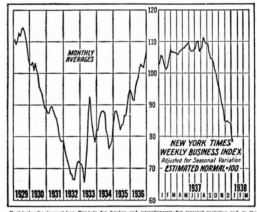

BUSINESS INDEX DROPS SHARPLY

Severest Loss Recorded, With Six Components Lower, Led by Heavy Declines in Power, Lumber and Loadings Series

Registering its sharpest loss, THE NEW YORK TIMES weekly index of business activity has dropped to 78.3 for the week ended Jan. 1, a decline of six points under the previous level of 84.3 (revised) and comparing with 103.0 for the corresponding week last year.

Six components were lower, led by particularly heavy weighted losses in electric power production, lumber output and miscellaneous carloadings. Power output declined more than seasonally. The seasonals for lumber and miscellaneous carloadings were higher but lumber production was sharply lower and cotton mill activity. The daily average for miscellaneous freight also dropped.

Smaller declines were recorded also for the automobile production series, "all other" carloadings and cotton mill activity. The only gain was furnished by the steel ingot component, production falling less than seasonally.

The following table gives the combined index and its components, each of which has been adjusted for seasonal variation and, in the case of carloadings, electric power production and cotton-mill activity, for long-term trend:

	Weeks Ended— Jan. 1, Dec. 25, Jan. 2, 1938. 1937. 1937
Combined index	78.3 *84.3 103.0
Miscel. car loadings	70.1 78.3 93.3
All other car loadings	84.2 90.4 88.0
Steel ingot production	37.5 35.9 122.2
Electric power prod.	103.4 *98.9 103.1
Automobile production	66.5 66.9 95.9
Lumber production	48.6 77.1 93.3
Cotton mill activity	76.4 83.7 140.8

*Revised, †Based on estimate of output.

NOTE.—Tables of working days and seasonal indices for 1938 have been compiled and may be obtained by addressing: Business News Department, THE NEW YORK TIMES, New York City.

Men and boys, women and girls stare at these and similar graphs in newspapers, read articles about the economic depression, or listen to stories told by their fellow workers in factories and offices. Many are afraid of losing their jobs, others of losing their savings and investments. Hence the schemes to offset the possibility of unemployment and of losses on the exchange. In such times of market depression well-to-do and working people are obsessed by the same fear.

Most workers live in constant fear of what their employers may do. Advertisements for hair dyes, means for removing wrinkles or preventing body odour, for making people attractive and young, strike home by picturing a boy or a girl saying: "The boss will fire me." Workers must be clean, good-looking, and not too old. In this connexion it does not matter whether an "age dead-line" is fixed which makes it necessary to dismiss a man of forty or fifty because he is too old. The quickening pace or finer specialization may work against the man who has reached middle age in factory or office. The resultant insecurity contributes to a social instability which in turn increases the chance of war and internal disturbances.

Many men deliberate not only on how to escape from their own personal difficulties but also on how to change the social order. Others favour aggressive action such as the persecution of the Jews in some countries of central Europe or attacks on foreigners who are held responsible for bad economic conditions. Party ideals influence daily life. In periods like the present the fear of war fuses together groups which have been antagonistic. Free discussion and calm judgment are not supported by governments in times of danger. Many peaceful activities were checked in almost all countries during the World War by espionage acts and other measures.

Nevertheless it must not be concluded that life in terrible times is full of misery and oppression. If men cannot remove the cause of their pain by direct means, they can often take refuge in friendship, love, poetry, or faith on the one hand, and in the calm of a scientific research, liberty of thought, and humanitarian effort. During the bloodiest years of the Renaissance the finest and noblest in man came to light. As aristocratic families in Perugia fought one another, masterpieces were painted in near-by Assisi. And before that Franciscans preached the simple life while armed men clashed.

Perhaps the oppressions and disturbances of today, the overstatements of political propaganda, and the unscientific attitude of the great public cause a strong inclination towards personal freedom and a scientific attitude as an overcompensation for the misery. "Civil liberty" was closely connected with the industrial revolution in spite of contemporaneous oppression. Men still yearn for it. As science develops, the conviction gains ground that social management would be more efficient if the scientific attitude were more generally held. The evidence is strong that a scientific attitude in modern daily life is increasing in spite of the difficulties that must be overcome; among these this human behaviour is an integral part of a certain social environment. We are all of us "conditioned" by tradition, by education, by social circumstance. Hence a scientific attitude is slowly acquired. It is well that this is so. For it is often dangerous for a nation to be forced to adopt rules at once instead of examining them again and again at leisure. The scientific attitude cannot be taught as arithmetic is taught. Protracted, comprehensive social and personal "training" is indispensable.

A scientific attitude cannot evolve in a vacuum, but must be based on the total traditional behaviour, a part of which is far from scientific. Social institutions may be changed and war and unemployment eliminated, but this does not instantly alter behaviour which is so ingrained in everybody that most men take it for granted and never give it a thought. Who ever asks why men wear trousers and women skirts in Western civilization; why horseflesh, snakes, and rats are not a part of our food;

130

why men are buried or cremated and not transformed into soap? Traditions and superstitions are still at work. Skyscrapers are symbols of modern cities, but:

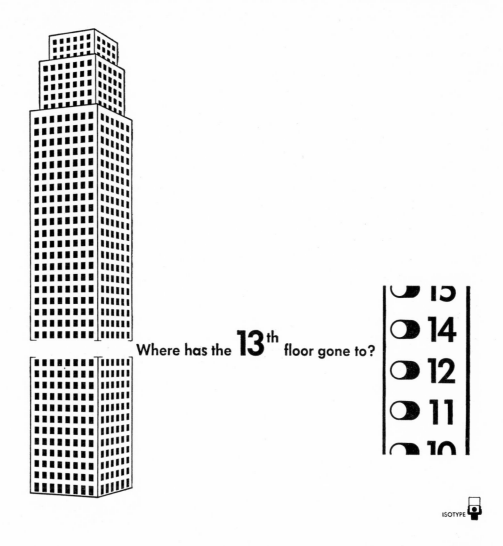

Where has the **13**th floor gone to?

ISOTYPE

The life of modern man is not wholly modern. The environment may be the last word in technology, but life itself is shot through and through with inherited ways of thinking and behaving that are centuries old. These are insufficiently analysed. During and immediately after the World War the number of books on spiritualism, astrology, and such subjects increased. Table-tipping, the materialization of spirits, clairvoyance, and remnants of demonology and thaumaturgy have their adherents. The superstitious taboo of the number thirteen is not unique. How many people knock on wood and believe in talismans and charms? Science must investigate this aspect of social behaviour and explain what part it plays in the social order as a whole. All nationalism, all social and personal ideals have their roots in ancient beliefs.

That scientists try to discuss these questions without bias may be called a trend towards modernity, but no scientist can avoid the influence of tradition when he begins his investigations. He is unconsciously encumbered by his own personal beliefs. Step by step these may be transformed. It is not unusual for reformers and revolutionaries to overstate the effects which can be achieved in the field of personal, religious, artistic, and scientific behaviour. Biological knowledge of today, with the theory of heredity, does not indicate whether science will be able to transform man by altering glands, by a certain personal "training," or by other measures.

The social order might be reconstructed without fundamentally changing human character, merely by transforming social institutions on the basis of traditional scientific attitude. Thus it may still be possible to love and hate one another, but with a sense of social security that is now lacking. New and grave human difficulties will then arise. But that problem is the concern of a more remote future. Without pursuing utopian ideals, men capable of judging themselves and their institutions scientifically should also be capable of widening the sphere of peaceful co-operation; for the historical record shows clearly enough that the trend has been in that direction on the whole and that the more co-operative man is, the more "modern" he is.

Appendix

The purpose of this appendix is to make certain additions and acknowledgments so that the reader may be stimulated to read various books, either as sources of great scientific value or as general and more popular works of information. Many special publications have been consulted.

For readers who are interested in the general statements and their sources it may be a help to thumb over the following comprehensive publications:

Statistical Year-Book of the League of Nations
World Economic Survey (League of Nations)
Annuaire internationale de statistique (Institut International de Statistique)
Aperçu de la démographie (Institut International de Statistique)
The Statesman's Year-Book (London)
Appendix, containing world surveys, of *Statistisches Jahrbuch für das Deutsche Reich*
Statistisches Handbuch der Weltwirtschaft (Berlin)
W. Woytinsky: *Die Welt in Zahlen* (Berlin, 1925)
M. G. Mulhall's *Dictionary of Statistics*
Isaac Lippincott: *Economic Resources and Industries of the World* (New York, 1930)
Publications of the World Power Conference
Statistical Abstracts of various countries, such as the United States, the United Kingdom, the British Empire, etc.
Handbooks, such as the *China Year-Book*, the *Chinese Year-Book*, the *Japan Year-Book*, the *South American Hand-Book*, the *Handbook of the Soviet Union*, and others
George Sarton: *Introduction to the History of Science* (Baltimore, 1927)
The Cambridge Ancient History

Several encyclopædias contain valuable material, such as the *Encyclopædia Britannica*. Newspapers and periodicals contain much vivid but not always reliable material.

Certain quotations are included as useful and stimulating, because they show how the generalizations of the kind made in this book can be based on detailed explanations and vivid descriptions. A book in which pictures and text are interwoven, as in this one, cannot compete with documented works. It is offered as a supplement or as an introduction to the subject of social man.

Page 7. ". . . based on the ISOTYPE method . . ."

The ISOTYPE method (see Otto Neurath: *International Picture Language, the First Rules of Isotype*; London, 1936) is founded on a special visual dictionary of about two thousand symbols and a special visual grammar which can be used to tell a story in pictures which can be understood almost at a glance. Machines, the functions of animals and men, plans of cities, social facts, and historical trends are explained by standardized elements which are put together like building-blocks to convey ideas and tell coherent stories.

The pedagogic value of this visual method has already been demonstrated in general education and in schools, in teaching lessons of public health, child care, safety, and so on, to adults and to children. With good visual aids, one is less dependent on good teachers. It is easy to interpret ISOTYPE pictures, but a period of training is necessary to compose them.

The selection of educational material is not so simple. The man who can leave things out most skilfully is the best teacher. The "transformation" of certain ideas into clear lay-outs based on the material selected is the second difficult step. Everything has to be reduced to its bones. It needs a special aptness to create a definitely satisfactory chart according to a given lay-out. Irrelevant details are ruled out. This applies not only to the separate symbols but also to the complete charts. The actors on this stage must work together, constantly influencing each other.

The ISOTYPE method may well become one of the elements that may help to bring about a civilization in which all men can participate in a common culture and in which the canyon between educated and uneducated will be bridged. Perhaps everyone will work as a specialist in his field; at the same time he will—he must—take part actively in the common life, understanding the main problems of his world and sharing in the responsibility for solving them. Our generation is opening the way for this new life of tomorrow in spite of all counteractions. Part of this preparation is the improvement in our means for cultural communication, which are already beginning to reshape our whole scheme of education. We cannot hope to democratize cultural life without many new ways of conveying information. One of these is the ISOTYPE method, which aims to provide a simple, comprehensive, and exact means of visualization.

Page 8. ". . . to take a scientific attitude . . ."

See John Dewey: "Unity of Science as a Social Problem," *International Encyclopedia of Unified Science*, Volume I, Number 1 (Chicago, 1938), p. 29. L. Susan Stebbing: *Thinking to Some Purpose* (Penguin Books, 1939).

Page 8. "Walt Whitman's 'There was . . .' "

    Walt Whitman: *Leaves of Grass.* See "Song of Myself."

Page 8. "Goethe's saying that 'a philistine . . .' "

    Wolfgang Goethe: *Zahme Xenien*, Sechste Reihe, 30.

"Was ist ein Philister?	"What is a Philistine?
Ein hohler Darm,	An empty sausage-skin,
Mit Furcht und Hoffnung ausgefüllt,	Stuffed with fear and hope,
Dass Gott erbarm!"	May God have mercy!"

Page 8. ". . . Walt Whitman's unceasing enthusiasm, 'the Modern Man I sing.' "

    Walt Whitman: *Leaves of Grass.* See "One's-self I sing."

Page 14. "The Black Death . . ."

    Hans Zinsser: *Rats, Lice and History* (Boston: Little, Brown & Company, 1935), page 88:

    "The Black Death, spreading in Europe . . . found an entirely susceptible population, which accounts for its terrific ravages. When its first sweep across the Continent was exhausted for want of victims, it remained endemic, smouldering until relighted by the accumulation of new fuel. . . . In 1899, isolated cases occurred in Trieste, Hamburg, Glasgow, Marseilles, and Naples. . . . As late as 1907, twenty-four Chinese of San Francisco came down with plague. . . . Yet no epidemics have resulted."

    M. Kowalewsky: *Die ökonomische Entwicklung Europas* (Berlin, 1911), Vol. V, page 341:

    "Since, as we have seen, serfdom had long since made room here for paid labour, the propertied Spanish classes seem particularly to have been affected by the devastation of resources and the increase in wages following the sudden drop in population on the Iberian Peninsula. For the influence of the Black Death made itself more poignantly felt here than in other European countries, in that the part-owners and tenants were suspending payment of their taxes in money and produce and the landed proprietors, in consequence of the demands for high wages, made increased use of the cheaper serf labour."

Page 14. ". . . kings and popes, painters and scientists . . ."

    For instance:
    1138. Lothar, the Holy Roman Emperor
    1270. Saint Louis, King of France

1438. Edward, King of Portugal
1457. Ladislaus, King of Bohemia and Hungary
1494. Ghirlandaio
1511. Giorgione
1523. Perugino
1576. Titian

Page 14. ". . . unemployment . . ."

The figures for the last two years are percentages of unemployment among insured persons. In the years for which the figures are available for trade-union members *and* for insured persons there was a considerable agreement between them:

AVERAGE YEARLY PERCENTAGES

	Trade-Union Members Unemployed Per Cent	Insured Persons Unemployed Per Cent
1922	15.2	16.1
1923	11.3	12.4
1924	8.1	10.8
1925	10.5	12.0
1926	12.2	13.2

See also *Abstract of Labor Statistics.*

Page 15. ". . . police kept the plague outside western and central Europe."

A. Proust: *La Défense de l'Europe contre la Peste* (Paris, 1897), page 271:
"During the plague of 1531 and 1533 the Parliament, in an ordinance dated August 26, 1531, laid down the measures to be taken. . . ."

Victor Heiser: *An American Doctor's Odyssey* (New York: W. W. Norton & Company; 1936), page 98:
"Bubonic plague, a name synonymous with disaster to the Ancient and Mediæval World, need not exist in the Modern. . . . Flea surveys are now made to show that species are present among the denizens of the rat underworld. A port may be considered non-infectible when the flea population of the average rat contains no more than one cheopis.

"New York is a safe port. The New Yorker may seek his Sabine Farm as a pleasant refuge, he need never be driven there by the blind panic which possessed the citizens of Florence when the Black Death had stormed their walls and taken their city in 'a sad and wonderful manner.' But the citizens of San Francisco, Mobile, and New Orleans must still exercise vigilance if they wish to sleep in peace."

Page 16. ". . . came from the steppes in Central Asia."

Source of the map: Studies of Professor Josef Strzygowski's institute for the history of arts at the University of Vienna.

Page 16. ". . . the Lop Nor lake . . . changed its position. . . ."

Sven Hedin: *Der wandernde See* (Leipzig, 1937).

Page 16. "Outer Mongolia . . ."

To the regions of Outer Mongolia the region of Tannu Tuva has been added, which is bounded by Outer Mongolia and by the Soviet Union. It was formerly considered part of Outer Mongolia but is now an independent republic under the protection of the Soviet Union.

Page 17. ". . . badly fed soldiers do not win battles."

The Times, London, March 11, 1938, page 8:

"Mr. Hore-Belisha's Speech: 'Out of every 100 boys who have passed through the Physical Development Depôt which my predecessor established 92 have passed into the Army as fully fitted soldiers. In view of the satisfactory results it is proposed to open at least one more physical development depôt in 1938. One of the items of diet on which recruits in the physical development depôt are sustained is, according to prevailing medical doctrine, milk. In future not only these recruits but all others who, in the opinion of the medical officer, need special nourishment will have an extra issue of half a pint of this stimulant a day.' "

Page 22. "The pre-Columbian civilization of America was highly developed. . . ."

See the usual reference books; also: Dr. Stephen-Chauvet: *L'Ile de Paques* (Paris, 1935).

Page 22. "The influence of the Arabic civilization . . ."

George Sarton: *Introduction to the History of Science* (Baltimore: Williams & Wilkins Company; 1927), Volume II, "From Rabbi Ben Ezra to Roger Bacon," Part I, page 32 ("Survey of Scientific Thought in the Twelfth and Thirteenth Centuries"):

"At any rate we may take the date 1144 as the date of introduction of Arabic alchemy into western Europe."

Page 22. ". . . peace for the sake of peace . . ."

> V. A. Smith: *The Early History of India* (Oxford University Press, 1924), pages 164, 185:
>
> "Inasmuch as the reign of Asoka lasted for fully forty years, he must have been a young man when, in or about the year 273 B.C., he undertook the government of the vast empire which had been won and kept by his grandfather and father. . . .
>
> "The victor records with sorrow that 150,000 persons were carried into captivity, 100,000 were slain, and that many times that number perished from famine, pestilence, and the other calamities which follow in the train of armies.
>
> "The sight of all this misery and the knowledge that he alone had caused it smote the conscience of Asoka, and awakened in his breast feelings of remorse, profound sorrow, and regret.
>
> "The king acted up to the principles which he professed, and abstained from aggressive war for the rest of his life. About this time he came under the influence of Buddhist teaching, his devotion to which increased more and more as the years rolled on. . . .
>
> "It is easy to understand that believers in ideas of this kind may be led logically to regard the life of an insect as entitled to no less respect than that of a man. In practice, indeed, the sanctity of animal was placed above that of human life; and the absurd spectacle was sometimes witnessed of a man being put to death for killing an animal, or even for eating meat. The most pious Buddhist and Jain kings had no hesitation about inflicting capital punishment upon their subjects, and Asoka himself continued to sanction the death penalty throughout his reign."

Page 25. "Silk Roads."

> Sven Hedin: *Die Seidenstrasse* (Leipzig, 1936).
> Albert Herrmann: *Die alten Seidenstrassen zwischen China und Syrien* (Berlin, 1910).

Page 27. "The Egyptians destroyed papyrus when too much of it grew . . ."

> Otto Neurath: *Antike Wirtschaftsgeschichte*, Chapter V, *"Das Griechisch-orientalische Wirtschaftssystem"* (Leipzig: B. G. Teubner, 3rd edition 1926).

Page 27. "The Mongols . . ."

> Harold Lamb: *Genghis Khan* (New York: Robert M. McBride & Company; 1927). A stimulating introduction.

Page 29. "After the first steps of conquest . . ."

> George Sarton: *Introduction to the History of Science*, Volume II, Part II, Chapter xxviii ("Survey of Science and Intellectual Progress in the First Half of the Thirteenth Century"), page 503:

"*Mongol and Chinese*—The great Conqueror, Chingiz Khan, deserves to be remembered in this survey on the same grounds as many other rulers who were not simply generals and statesmen but cultural promoters of the very first order. . . . We may speak of a Mongol civilization originated by Chingiz Khan, which was essentially a combination of elements derived from China, Central Asia, and Islam, and adapted to their own needs. He showed much toleration of foreign faiths."

Chapter xlii ("Survey of Science and Intellectual Progress in the Second Half of the Thirteenth Century"), page 726:

"*China and Mongolia*—It is hardly necessary to insist upon the immense educational task accomplished by Kublai Khan. In a sense everything was to be done for his Mongolian subjects, and he did the most difficult part, the beginning."

Page 30. "The Treaty of Westphalia . . ."

The Treaty of Westphalia consists of two treaties, one between the German Emperor and France, the other between the German Emperor and Sweden. The Netherlands and Switzerland were declared independent.

Page 31. "Congress of Vienna."

The Ottoman Empire is excluded from the European states. This is an old tradition. The ideas of world unity of Erasmus (Dutch scholar, 1467–1536) excluded the Turks. Leibnitz (German scientist, 1646–1716) suggested that the French King fight the Turks instead of fighting Austria.

At the Congress of Vienna European problems were predominant. The question of Negro slavery and the settling of difficulties in Guiana, however, were also discussed. The map does not show extra-European dependencies of the signatory powers.

Page 31. "Treaties of Versailles, Saint-Germain, Trianon."

Treaties signed by the Allies after the World War are:
Treaty of Versailles (with Germany)
Treaty of Saint-Germain (with Austria and Czechoslovakia)
Treaty of Trianon (with Hungary)
Treaty of Neuilly (with Bulgaria)
Treaty of Lausanne (with Turkey).

In the chart the Treaty of Brest-Litovsk, between the Soviet Union and the Central Powers, has been included.

Page 32. "After the conquest . . ."

Use William H. Prescott's books as introductions, and Philip Ainsworth Means: *Fall of the Inca Empire* (New York and London: Charles Scribner's Sons; 1932).

Page 34. ". . . 'This dark Madonna was the heathen goddess Tonantzin . . .' "

Richard Summers: *Dark Madonna* (Caldwell, Idaho: Caxton Printers; 1937).

Page 34. ". . . they needed Indian wives . . ."

Philip Ainsworth Means: *Fall of the Inca Empire,* page 69:
"Not only did the physical hardships and the inevitable perils incidental to going to Peru deter many Spanish women from accompanying their husbands, and lead them to quaint subterfuges to avoid it, but also the law tended to discourage the growth of a Spanish female population in Peru not alone by prohibiting the going thither of unmarried women but also by authorizing marriage between Spanish men and Christianized native women. . . . The mixture of blood was not necessarily a bad one; indeed, such men as Father Blas Valera and the Inca Garcilaso de la Vega prove that it could be a very good one. At all events, the mestizos of Peru came to form a large and important class in colonial society. Subsequently, as we shall see further on, greater numbers of Spanish women came into the country and helped in the formation of its small but powerful pure white uppermost class."

Page 34. ". . . this new slavery . . ."

Thomas Clarkson: *History of the Rise, Progress and Accomplishment of the Abolition of the African Slave Trade by the British Parliament* (London, 1839).
L. C. Vrijman: *Slavenhalers en slavenhandel* (Amsterdam, 1937).
Thomas F. Buxton: *The African Slave Trade* (London, 1840).
Abram L. Harris: *The Negro as Capitalist* (Philadelphia: American Academy of Social and Political Science; 1936), page ix.

Page 36. ". . . the division of the earth between the Spanish and Portuguese . . ."

Petermann's Mitteilungen, September 1937, page 83.

Page 39. ". . . pirates . . ."

Philip Gosse: *The History of Piracy* (New York: Longmans, Green & Company; 1932).
Pages 307–8 ("The Classical Pirates") : ". . . Pompey . . .
"In forty days after his arrival off the coast of Asia Minor, the pirates were completely crushed . . . four hundred ships had been captured, thirteen hundred destroyed, all arsenals burnt, and all forts razed. More than ten thousand pirates were computed to have been drowned and twenty thousand captured."

Page 39. "They went . . . where they found the most wealth and the least resistance."

Rolf Nordenstreng: *Die Züge der Wikinger* (Leipzig, 1925).
Axel Olrik: *Viking Civilization* (New York: W. W. Norton & Company; 1930).

Allen Mawer: *The Vikings* (New York: G. P. Putnam's Sons; 1913).

George Sarton: *Introduction to the History of Science*, Vol. I, page 724 ("The Time of Al-Biruni. First Half of Eleventh Century").

Matthias Thórdarson: *The Vinland Voyages* (New York: American Geographical Society; 1930).

Page 41. ". . . the Irish question . . ."

Mary Hayden and George A. Moonan: *A Short History of the Irish People* (London and New York: Longmans, Green & Company; 1922).

Page 41. ". . . a series of names appears representing . . ."

Treaty of Peace between the Allied and Associated Powers and Germany. Signed at Versailles, June 28th, 1919 (British Foreign Office. H.M. Stationery Office, 1925):

"For this purpose the HIGH CONTRACTING PARTIES represented as follows:

HIS MAJESTY THE KING OF THE UNITED KINGDOM OF GREAT BRITAIN AND IRELAND AND OF THE BRITISH DOMINIONS BEYOND THE SEAS, EMPEROR OF INDIA . . .

and

for the DOMINION OF CANADA . . .

for the COMMONWEALTH OF AUSTRALIA . . .

for the UNION OF SOUTH AFRICA . . .

for the DOMINION OF NEW ZEALAND . . .

for INDIA . . ."

Page 41. ". . . every self-governing member of the Empire is master of its destiny . . ."

For a similar formula see *Constitution of the Union of Soviet Socialist Republics* (Moscow: Co-operative Publishing Society of Foreign Workers in the U.S.S.R.; 1936), Article 17.

"For each Union Republic is reserved the right freely to secede from the U.S.S.R."

Page 41. "This is the British Commonwealth of Nations."

The Cambridge History of the British Empire (New York: The Macmillan Company; 1929), Volume I, "The Old Empire from the Beginnings to 1783," pages v, 20:

". . . It was not until late in the fifteenth century that her oceanic expansion began. . . .

"If anything absolutely new can be traced to the possession of our Empire, it must be traced to the most original feature in it, the progressive develop-

ment of dependencies into independent partner nations which have nevertheless remained by the mother country's side and under the same sovereign."
K. C. Wheare: *The Statute of Westminster and Dominion Status* (Oxford University Press, 1938).

Page 45. ". . . modernity."

See a vivid picture of a city moving towards modernity in Robert S. and
Helen Lynd: *Middletown* (New York: Harcourt, Brace & Company; 1929) and
Middletown in Transition (1937).

Middletown, page v: "the realities of social science are what people do";
page vi: "the social anthropology of contemporary life"; page 4: "the life of
the people as a unit complex of interwoven trends of behavior."

Page 46. "Birth-rate."

T. H. Marshall, R. Kuczynski, and others: *The Population Problem* (London: George Allen & Unwin; 1938).

T. H. Marshall: "What the Public Thinks," page 32:
"The general view was that people will always want children. Deliberately
childless marriages occur, and more often, we were told, in the middle than in
the working-class. But they are exceptional. And what is the upper limit? . . .

"It would seem that forces over which politicians and economists can exercise no control have determined that few mothers to-day are willing to have
more than three children. Whatever we do, it is extremely unlikely that we
shall go back to the large families of the last century."

R. Kuczynski: "World Population," pages 107, 112, 119:
"In 1770 the average length of a white person's life was about thirty years.
Now it is about sixty years. Before this reduction of mortality began, the white
population of the world was not increasing; births were only just sufficient to
fill the gaps caused by deaths. Since that time births have exceeded deaths in
almost every single year, and the population has increased continuously. . . .

"That the Italian and the German Governments themselves consider their
population policies as inadequate is proven by the fact that they have recently
announced emphatically the necessity of taking new measures."
A. M. Carr-Saunders: *World Population* (Oxford University Press; 1936).
D. V. Glass: *The Struggle for Population* (Oxford University Press; 1936).

Page 52. "The Chinese developed methods of intensive use of the soil . . ."

K. A. Wittfogel: *Wirtschaft und Gesellschaft Chinas* (Leipzig, 1931), page
303:
"At the beginning of the Chou dynasty, of the twelfth century B.C., nothing

144

was yet known of a general fertilization of the fields. Then only the seeds were fertilized. . . . Thereby was one stage in the intensification of agriculture achieved—one which India did not attain until modern times, not to mention the agriculture of pre-industrial Europe. In the second great epoch of Chinese history, during that time when the north of the Great Plain was cultivated, the technique of fertilizing was also manifestly developed from a treatment of seeds alone to the complete one of the soil itself."

Page 54. "A new life, with more leisure, began."

> H. M. Vernon: *The Shorter Working Week* (London: George Routledge & Sons; 1934).

Page 55. ". . . symptom of modernity."

> The discussion of cultural trends is a scientific tradition.
> See Adolphe Quételet: *Physique sociale ou Essai sur le développement des facultés de l'homme* (Brussels and Paris, 1869), Vol. II, p. 152, "Development of the Intellectual Faculties"; p. 171, "Postal Service and Electric Telegraphs"; p. 232, "Suicides and Duels"; p. 388, "The Average Man Considered with Respect to Philosophy and Morals"; p. 389, "Laws of the Development of Humanity." Without discussing the basic principles of certain ideas dealing with "evolution," the stimulating book of Alfredo Niceforo: *Les Indices numériques de la civilisation et du progrès* (Paris, 1921), might also be mentioned.

Page 55. ". . . philosophers hesitated to speak freely about suicide."

> When David Hume (1711–76) was preparing a volume of his essays for publication in 1757, he removed two of these essays from the copies which were already printed and had to add other text in place of them. He did so out of respect for public opinion and that of his friends. The text of the two essays was left in one of the original copies and was published after Hume's death: *Essays on Suicide and the Immortality of the Soul, ascribed to the late David Hume* (London, 1783). See J. H. Burton: *Life and Correspondence of David Hume* (Edinburgh, 1846, 1850) and Anton Thomson: *David Hume, sein Leben und seine Philosophie* (Berlin, 1912), Vol. I, page 95.

Page 61. "Silhouettes."

> "Silhouettes" are used to present simplified features of different countries. One country may be more "modern" than another in one field and less "modern" in other fields. Hence different countries cannot be ranked according to a single "degree of modernity." There is no satisfactory basis on which to compute the scale of the single elements of the silhouettes, such as length of life,

suicide-rate, literacy, number of radio sets, which would result in one "index number" of modernity for each country.

The data for this chart are the latest available (1935). Data for suicide and literacy are not identical with those for page 55. The span of life is a little longer for women than for men (see age groups, page 58). For Spain the last data available are for 1908–23. The figure has been expanded in proportion to the average of prolongation of life since then. In Japan literacy is higher than in some European countries. Elementary education is compulsory and school attendance has been high since the beginning of the twentieth century. *The Encyclopædia Britannica* (fourteenth edition, 1929) states: "Now there is practically no illiteracy" (see article "Japan," Vol. XII, p. 925). On the other hand, in the article "Illiteracy" (Vol. XII, p. 94) the same encyclopædia gives 4.3 per cent for illiteracy among the army conscripts in Japan.

Page 65. Chart: Economic Scheme.

The chart represents the approximate proportions between the number of workers in the different occupations who provide everything that the whole population uses, under the present technical conditions in an industrialized country. The population occupied in so doing appears once more (in outline) among the consuming population. Part of the population which belongs to the same age groups as those in occupations is not included in the Economic Scheme—for instance, students and housewives (though the latter play a not negligible part in the apportionment of consumption; the Russian statistics include them among those occupied). Other groups who only appear among the consumers are young people who are not yet occupied and old people who are no longer occupied.

The occupations represented are:

Use of natural resources: agriculture and stock-raising; forestry; fishing; extraction of minerals, stones, and earth; water-power.

Semi-manufacturing: textile industry; tanneries; flour and grain mills; lumber industries; chemical and allied industries; blast furnaces and steel rolling mills; clay, glass, and stone industries; gas, electricity, water-supply.

Manufacturing: clothing and millinery industries; shoemaking; food, beverage, cigar industries; paper industry, printing, and publishing; furniture-making; building trades; machine and other metal industries; shipbuilding; production of vehicles and aircraft.

Distribution and service: commerce; postal service; transport; education and recreation; health service; justice, police, army, and navy; domestic and personal service.

Page 65–6. "Such a scheme leads to the question . . ."

This agglomeration forms not only the environment of men's life, but also its fluctuations. Some think it should be possible to find *the* best environment, but others understand very well that a complete knowledge of all these details

146

opens up more than one choice. Men have always to decide whether they want to create some combination of production and accomplishments or not. Science can indicate certain broad plans and may help the choice in such a way, but it is not in a position to substitute for the choice "the best" solution.

One might demonstrate "silhouettes" of various combinations. At present there seems to be no way to calculate "maxima" or "optima" by means of index numbers representing different combinations of food and drink, shelter and recreation, building of houses, schools, theatres, together with the burden of working time, accidents, diseases, etc. The only way to aid conscious decisions is to clear the situation by comparing silhouettes.

Page 67. ". . . Southern workers."

Fernunterricht (Correspondence Course) (Vienna: Gesellschafts- und Wirtschaftsmuseum; 1931), Volume I, Number 2, page 6:

BRITISH INDIA: REAL WAGES, INCOME 1930

	Average yearly earnings in rupees	*Real wages and income in units of buying-power*
Wages of Labour in England, average £170	2300	100
Farmers	150	6
High-salaried Specialists (mechanics, locomotive engineers)	1200	50
Skilled Industrial Workers, low-paid category (weavers)	300	12
Unskilled Industrial Workers	120	5

Page 68. Chart: Sources of Power.

In order to make a combination of coal, petroleum, and water-power possible, a rough calculation has been made of how much energy may be produced from water-power during a year. The method adopted by the World Power Conference has been taken as a basis.

Page 71. ". . . Countries may be divided into overcrowded, crowded, and more or less empty ones."

This definition of "crowded" and "overcrowded" avoids the concept of an "optimum population." Such concepts cannot be sufficiently defined for scientific purposes and are not necessary for the decisions of men. Here again the method of "silhouettes" is preferable; such a discussion as the following becomes superfluous:

A. M. Carr-Saunders: *World Population* (Oxford University Press, 1936), page 330:

"The statement that, with reference to any given area, the optimum population is that population which produces maximum economic welfare is unexceptionable. Maximum economic welfare is not necessarily the same as maximum real income per head; but for practical purposes they may be taken as equivalent. Overpopulation exists when numbers exceed the optimum, and underpopulation when they fall below it; in either case real income per head is less than it would be if the optimum prevailed."

Naturally, importation is always possible; therefore the establishment of welfare depends upon the world situation, including social order, accidents, and disease. The term "maximum economic welfare" is not adequately defined.

Page 71. Chart: Area per Capita in Countries around the Pacific.

The area includes waste land, which forms a large part of Australia and also of China. The parts of Canada to the north of 60° have been separated from the rest. These parts can hardly sustain any population whatever.

Page 72. ". . . economics of humanity."

This term has been suggested by the sociologist Rudolf Goldscheid.

Page 73. "Now hundreds of thousands of expatriates live in foreign countries."

Among organizations which occupy themselves with the problems of emigrants are: the Nansen International Office for Refugees (especially for emigrants from Russia and for Armenians), the Intergovernmental Advisory Commission for Refugees, 1933, both under the authority of the League of Nations, and the permanent commission created by the intergovernmental conference of Évian, July 1938.

Page 74. "Fluctuations . . . may also arise in the Soviet Union . . . ."

SOVIET UNION

	Production of			Stocks of	
	Coal	Petroleum		Cattle	Pigs
	(millions of metric tons)			(millions)	
1920	8.6	3.8		34.2	14.5
1921	8.5	4.0		35.5	13.3
1922	9.0	4.9		32.3	6.0
1923	10.8	5.7		41.3	9.4
1924	16.2	6.5		47.6	17.2
1925	17.0	7.5		60.6	18.8
1926	26.0	8.8		64.1	18.1
1927	32.3	11.0		67.8	20.0
1928	35.8	12.3		70.5	26.0
1929	41.7	14.5		67.1	20.4
1930	47.1	18.6		52.5	13.6
1931	58.0	22.3		47.9	14.4
1932	64.4	21.4		40.7	11.6
1933	76.0	21.4		38.4	12.1
1934	93.9	24.2		42.4	17.5
1935	108.9	25.2		49.3	22.6
1936	126.2	27.3		56.5	30.4
1937	122.5	27.7	(1938)	50.9	25.7

Fluctuations in these figures in the years 1929–34 are due to collectivization.

Page 74. "Business cycles . . . become more and more international."

W. C. Mitchell: *Business Cycles* (New York: National Bureau of Economic Research; 1927), page 443:

"Another way of summing up the international relationships of business cycles since 1890 is to run down the columns of entries in table 32 for each year. There is no year of the 36 covered in which the same phase of the cycle prevailed in all of the 17 countries. Uniformity is approached, however, in 1893, 1899, 1906, 1908, 1912, 1916, 1920, and 1921; and in most years there is a marked preponderance of entries of similar tenor. . . . The existence of a general trend toward uniformity of business fortunes is plain."

Page 77. ". . . the possibilities of production and reconstruction are enormous. . . ."

Otto Neurath: "The Present Growth of World Productive Capacity" (The Hague, 1932) (Synopsis), page 751. See also page 105. In:

World Social Economic Planning. Material Contributed to the World Social Economic Congress, Amsterdam, August 1931. Published by the International Industrial Relations Institute. M. L. Fledderus, editor.

Page 78. "During the war many ships were lost . . ."

	Gross tonnage launched (millions)	Gross tonnage destroyed (millions)
1912–16	12.3	6.8
1917–21	26.2	11.4
1922–26	10.7	2.5
1927–31	12.3	5.5
1932–36	5.6	9.4

Page 81. "Autarchy . . ."

Otto Blum: *Verkehrsgeographie* (Berlin, 1936), page 47:

"Since the large countries always extend through diverse zones, the danger exists that the cooler areas which make up the political and economic centre of the state are imperilled first in their farming and then in their industry by the warmer areas, since the latter can produce many things more cheaply and because their population has a lower standard of living. So the white Northern states of the United States are endangered by the coloured Southern states. In the same way France, and especially the French farmer, is affected by Algeria. The fault lies particularly in transportation, which is too cheap and too rapid. What would happen to the German farmer if he were to live in a 'large country' and did not enjoy tariff protection?"

This is characteristic of certain kinds of argument used by promoters of autarchy.

Page 82. "novels and articles in periodicals dealing with such subjects."

Frank C. Hanighen: *The Secret War* (New York: John Day Co.; 1934), a journalist's book, partly based on Zischka's book on oil, and on J. K. Winkler: *W. R. Hearst, An American Phenomenon* (New York: Simon & Schuster; 1928), Anton Mohr: *The Oil War* (New York: Harcourt, Brace & Company; 1926), Pierre l'Espagnol de la Tramerye: *The World-Struggle for Oil* (New York: Alfred A. Knopf; 1924), Louis Fischer: *Oil Imperialism* (New York: International Publishers Co.; 1926), and other popular "unmasking" books. Other examples are: Ludwell Denny: *America Conquers Britain* (New York: Alfred A. Knopf; 1930), Ludwell Denny: *We Fight for Oil* (New York: Alfred A. Knopf; 1928), Sidney Russell Cooke and E. H. Davenport: *The Oil Trusts and Anglo-American Relations* (New York: The Macmillan Company; 1923).

Howard and Ralph Wolf: *Rubber* (New York: Covici Friede; 1936), pages 129, 130:

"The story of Africa's rubber monarch has been told. This is the story of the subjects, of the Congo blacks on whose stinking backs the tinpot King at Brussels mounted from virtual bankruptcy to the imperial magnificence of rubber sovereignty and a place among the real rulers of the world. Leopold himself never saw these blacks. . . .

"On soldier- and laborer-recruiting raids led by white officers troops 'regular' and irregular shot down defenseless blacks, struck down babies with gun butts, finished up with cannibal banquets. On punitive expeditions from major stations and from lost one-white outposts in the bush they went out unsupervised by white officer or agent to wreak vengeance on villages negligent in feeding rubber to Leopold and food to his gunmen, wood choppers, laborers and station slaves. Smoked hands they brought in by the basket in proof of orders obeyed and to demonstrate there had been no undue waste of ammunition. Sometimes male sexual organs were required, but if it was a showing of hands no questions were asked even if they had been sliced from children. In each of the rubber-gathering villages one or more of these cannibal riflemen was stationed as a sentry living on the people and driving all adult males into the forests to glean caoutchouc."

Page 83. ". . . the strength of both sides does not vary greatly."

During the World War the proportion between total mobilized troops and total population was about the same for all European nations involved (about twenty per cent). For Great Britain and France, however, there came troops from other parts of the world, which have been included. For the charts on the two following pages the assumption has been made that the proportion between the armies is the same as the proportion between the populations of the European territories. But for natural resources all the resources from overseas have been included; that is, Indian, Canadian, Australian, etc., for Great Britain, the resources of the total French Empire for France, etc.

150

Page 83. ". . . raw materials which are of importance for armament . . ."

> Alfred Plummer: *Raw Materials or War Materials?* (London: Victor Gollancz; 1937), page 11:
> "When, therefore, it is asserted that certain nations, countries or powers have not free access to raw materials, does this mean that they have difficulty in obtaining raw materials in peace time, or does it mean that they would have difficulty in obtaining them if they were at war? Or is it alleged that in both peace and war there is no free access to raw materials?"

Pages 84 and 85. Charts: Silhouettes of War Economy.

> It seems useful to show a selection of raw materials essential for waging war available to various alliances, instead of analysing the position of the "Big Seven" (see Frank H. Simonds and Brooks Emeny: *The Price of Peace* [New York: Harper & Brothers; 1935] and others) or of ranking the powers (see Herman Kranold: *The International Distribution of Raw Materials* [London: George Routledge & Sons; 1938], who uses index numbers in addition).
>
> Since this account is for the general reader, no fine distinctions have been made. The principle of calculation is this: The maximum of production since 1929 (that is mostly the production of 1929 or the latest year) has been considered for every country. This is because productive capacity is the essential point. Therefore the percentages differ from those of Kranold, who takes the average of the production of the most recent years, which depends on business conditions and does not give an impression of productive capacity. Sometimes estimates were necessary (for example, for rice-production in China, which is not zero, though it does not appear in most international statistics). The countries which are not belligerent can hardly be called "neutrals"; it has been assumed that their goods are divided among both belligerent parties, partly by trade, partly by occupation.
>
> No estimate has been attempted of possible petroleum-production. The "Big Seven" will be interested in the control of petroleum-production in the region of the Gulf of Mexico and the Caribbean, in the East Indies, and in the Near and Middle East.
>
> These rough outlines do not comprehend the question of substitutes for rubber, etc.

Page 87. Chart: Seasonal Fluctuations.

> See Mary Van Kleeck: *Miners and Management* (New York: Russell Sage Foundation; 1934), Part II, "The Problem of Coal in the United States; a record of failure and a forecast of the solution," page 184, "Coal in the Economic Crisis."

Page 87. "At present preparation for war often reduces unemployment and stimulates production."

> Joseph Lowe: *The Present State of England* (Second Edition, London, 1823):
> Page 31, "Increase of Employment during the War . . ."
> Page 33, ". . . we have merely to refer them to a comparison of the average rate of wages and salaries in particular periods, such as 1792 and 1812; to the increased sales of our manufacturers and merchants, the rise of rent to the landlord; the increase of profit to his tenant."

Page 88. Chart: Pax Romana.

> See, for instance, *The Cambridge Ancient History*, Vol. XI, "The Imperial Peace" (New York: The Macmillan Company; 1936) and James H. Breasted: *The Conquest of Civilization* (New York: Harper & Brothers; 1926).
> Pitrim A. Sorokin's *Social and Cultural Dynamics* (New York: American Book Company; 1937), Volume III, "Fluctuation of Social Relationships, War, and Revolution," contains valuable and stimulating statistical material concerning war in history. This is not the place to discuss statements such as (pages 377–8, 342):
> "A study of all the compartments of culture of Greece has shown that the fifth and the fourth centuries B.C. were the periods of transition from Ideational to Sensate culture, in the history of Greece, while, beginning with the third century, Sensate culture became more or less crystallized and dominant there. . . . The fourth and the fifth centuries were the most belligerent centuries in Greek history. In the third and then in the second centuries, the curve of war falls sharply. . . . Turn now to the curve of Rome. . . . The third century gives a sudden and an enormous rise of war. It is the most militant century in Roman history. Though the Roman culture began possibly to disintegrate somewhat in that century, the disintegration was not so great as to warrant such a rise of war magnitude. In other words, the rise of the war curve in that century may be explained by the interference of other factors than the transition discussed. . . . This rise of war curve . . . can be accounted for through the Carthaginian invasion rather than by the factor of transition. . . . The first century A.D. is the century of a comparatively crystallized Sensate culture. Respectively, the war indicator for it is very low. . . . Low remains also the indicator for the second century, though it is higher than for the first (in absolute figures). In that century the Sensate culture began to be undermined, but not very much, as yet. The third century is definitely the century of transition from the Sensate to the coming Ideational culture. Exactly in accordance with the hypothesis, the curve of war rises notably. . . .
> "If now we take the relative indicators of the casualties, probably the most important criterion of war, they tell definitely and unequivocally that the curse of privilege to be the most devastating or the most bloody war century belongs to the twentieth; in one quarter century it imposed upon the population a 'blood tribute' far greater than that imposed by any of the whole

centuries compared [i.e., twelfth to twentieth centuries]. The next place belongs to the seventeenth, and then comes the eighteenth century; the nineteenth century appears to be the least bloody of all these centuries concerned. . . ."

Page 89. ". . . cruelty in peace-time."

In peace-time people learn quickly all kinds of cruelty. See, for instance, George Allan England: *Vikings of the Ice* (Garden City, N. Y.: Doubleday, Page & Company; 1924):

". . . On deck, louder yells summoned. Keen with the blood lust, all who could go on the ice began heaving on their gear. Such a shouting, such a leaping to arms, such a buckling-on of sheath knives, steels, belts, such a grabbing of tow ropes and murderous gaffs you never could imagine.

". . . From the bridge I hear the Old Man again: 'I hate to kill these seal, I do, indeed. It fair pains me!' Astonishment! Has the Cap'n gone mad or turned tenderhearted? Neither. For now he adds: 'They're so wonderful small; some of them hardly worth the bother. If they could only have been let grow another week. . . .'

". . . The kill draws to its close for lack of killable material. . . ."

Page 94. Chart: Profile of Family Income in Columbia, South Carolina, 1933.

See *Consumer Use of Selected Goods and Services by Income Classes*, Market Research Series, prepared by the United States Department of Commerce, 1935 and 1936. The income groups represented are sample families, taken from the whole of the population in a proportion which is as nearly as possible that of the groups to the whole population.

Page 95. ". . . the hoboes . . ."

Nels Anderson: *The Hobo* (Chicago: University of Chicago Press; 1923), Preface and pages 3, 14, 61:

"The man whose restless disposition made him a pioneer on the frontier tends to become a 'homeless man'—a hobo and a vagrant—in the modern city. From the point of view of their biological predispositions, the pioneer and the hobo are perhaps the same temperamental type; from the point of view of their socially acquired traits, they are something quite different. . . .

"A survey of the lodging-house and hotel population, supplemented by the census reports of the areas in which they live, indicates that the number of homeless men in Chicago ranges from 30,000 in good times to 75,000 in hard times.

"From the records and observations of a great many men the reasons why men leave home seem to fall under several heads: (a) seasonal work and unemployment, (b) industrial inadequacy, (c) defects of personality, (d) crises in the life of the person, (e) racial or national discrimination, and (f) wanderlust."

Pages 96–7. Charts: Two Types of Tenements, and Living-Conditions and Mortality from Tuberculosis in Brooklyn.

> See the publications of the State Board of Housing, New York, of the Department of Health, New York, the maps and charts prepared by the Slum Clearance Committee, New York, and Robert S. and Helen Lynd: *Middletown* and *Middletown in Transition*.

Page 98. "Most marriages are between persons of the same social standing."

> See statistical material in Alfredo Niceforo's *Anthropologie der nichtbesitzenden Klassen*.

Page 100. ". . . dissatisfaction . . . expressed freely."

> Nels Anderson: *The Hobo* (Chicago: University of Chicago Press; 1923), pages 229, 228:
> "What of the soap-box reformer and revolutionist? Is he a menace or merely a joke? The curbstone orator is not an agitator in the ordinary sense of that word. He is merely a thinking hobo. . . .
> "Soap-boxers all say that they have enjoyed more liberty in Chicago than in most cities. Chicago police have always taken a generous and liberal attitude toward the curbstone forum."

Pages 101–2. ". . . relatively minor disturbances ended by changing the social and political order."

> In connexion with this it should be mentioned that groups of zealous and convinced adherents of an idea are generally small, and that the great majority of people have no serious conviction and adhere to the victorious. Macaulay is of the same opinion and gives an example:
> Thomas Babington Macaulay: *Critical and Historical Essays*, "Burleigh and His Times":
> "There was undoubtedly a zealous Protestant party and a zealous Catholic party. But both these parties were, we believe, very small. We doubt whether both together made up, at the time of Mary's death, the twentieth part of the nation. The remaining nineteen twentieths halted between the two opinions, and were not disposed to risk a revolution in the government, for the purpose of giving to either of the extreme factions an advantage over the other. . . .
> "Those risings clearly showed how small and feeble both the parties were. Both in the one case and in the other the nation ranged itself on the side of the government, and the insurgents were speedily put down and punished."

Page 103. "Irrigation is important . . . in . . . China."

> See Chao-ting Chi: *Key Economic Areas in Chinese History* (New York: Peter Smith; 1936) and K. A. Wittfogel: *Wirtschaft und Gesellschaft Chinas* (Leipzig, 1931).

Page 103. ". . . gigantic dams are built . . ."

> Among other plans is that of cultivating the Sahara, by creating a higher level of water in the Mediterranean.

Pages 104–5. Charts: The Basin of the Mississippi and Its Tributaries, The Flooded Area near the Estuary of the Mississippi and Its Population.

> See *The Mississippi Valley Flood Disaster of 1927*, Official Report of the Relief Operations, The American Red Cross, Washington, D. C., October 1929.

Page 106. ". . . the exhaustion of the soil . . ."

> See *Second Report of the Science Advisory Board* (Washington, D. C., 1935), W. L. G. Joerg: "Research Problems in Natural Science Bearing on National Land Planning," pages 381, 388:
>
> "The most important physical crisis in land use is soil erosion. . . . The Soil Erosion Service has been established. It has three principal functions: to investigate the process and causes of soil wastage, to record the areal extent and severity of surface destruction, and to undertake protective management of slopes to stop such losses and restore normal conditions. A fully successful campaign of soil and surface conservation must rest on a knowledge of the process of soil wastage and its areal expressions. This knowledge is derived from two types of studies, one dealing with climate and the other with the relation of soil to slope. . . .
>
> "The most important project under the head of vegetation, however, is possibly the study of the genetics of the domesticated plants native to America with regard to their directed breeding. . . ."

Page 109. ". . . or to overcome the disadvantages of . . . climate."

> Ellsworth Huntington: *The Pulse of Asia* (Boston: Houghton, Mifflin Co.; 1907), Preface and pages 362, 382, 383, 384:
>
> "At the beginning of the Christian era, the vast plains of Central Asia appear to have supported untold hordes of nomads. When the plains began to grow rapidly drier, the inhabitants must have suffered sorely.
>
> "As the nomads pressed outward from the drier central regions of Asia, we can imagine how they were obliged to fight with the neighboring tribes

whom they tried to dispossess. The old inhabitants and the newcomers could not all live together; new migrations would be a necessity; and confusion would spread in every direction. Meanwhile, Europe, after its long period of blighting cold, was becoming warm and habitable, and the migrants pressed into it, horde after horde. No one tribe could stay long in its chosen abiding-place, for new bands of restless nomads pressed upon it. Rome fell before the wanderers. Nothing could stay their progress until the turn of the tide. . . ."

Page 116. Chart: Work, Leisure, Sleep.

"Three times eight hours" seems to be an old and world-wide tradition. Alexandra David-Neel: *With Mystics and Magicians in Tibet* (London: Penguin Books; 1937), page 89: "The daily routine included eight hours of meditation divided in four periods of two hours—eight hours of study and manual work—eight hours devoted to sleep, meals and recreation according to individual tastes."

H. M. Vernon: *The Shorter Working Week* (London: George Routledge & Sons; 1934), page 168:

". . . There is usually a good deal of similarity in the leisure-hour occupations of persons of the same social class who are living in the same district and are employed on somewhat similar types of industrial work. . . . An investigation is described in the . . . report on New Aspects of the Problem of Hours of Work . . . men and women in Liverpool. . . .

AVERAGE DISTRIBUTION OF TOTAL HOURS PER WEEK

	Men	Women
At work	48	48
In transit to or from work	9	9
Meals and personal matters	21	21
Sleep	55	60
Balance of leisure	35	30
Total hours in the week	168	168

. . . All the persons interrogated spent some portion of their time on amusements and recreations, and the table indicates that 72 per cent of the men and women spent over three hours each in attending religious services."

Page 117. "Becoming . . . fit through exercise is accepted on principle in Great Britain. . . ."

In the "Keep Fit" movement the Britons coin slogans such as "Throughout the Empire in work or play fitness wins." National fitness has become a state policy and physical training the subject of the national health campaign. One can find similar tendencies in almost all countries, in the United States, the Soviet Union, Australia, and Japan.

Page 118. "Armies are the embodiment of businesslike practice on the one hand (through the progressive elimination from soldiers' drill . . .)"

The advertising appeal is very attractive: "The Army is a good job."

Page 125. Chart: Features of Death.

To show the importance of infant mortality in the question of health, the number of deaths of infants needs to be compared with the number of new-born children. In this chapter and in this chart mortality in general is considered, to show how often a modern man is likely to be afflicted by the death of a fellow human being.

Page 126. "How can one test the state of religion?"

Robert S. and Helen Merrell Lynd: *Middletown* (New York: Harcourt, Brace & Company; 1929), pages 382, 393, 396:
"The usual prayer meeting in the largest Middletown churches consists of twenty-five to fifty persons, the large majority of them adults over forty, with women predominating as in the Sunday services. A new Minister in the largest church in Middletown succeeded in raising the attendance temporarily to 150 by reducing the usual prayer meeting to half an hour and following it with a more informal discussion meeting. . . . The Sunday School is the chief instrument of the church for training the young in religion; of secondary importance is the 'young people's society' meeting in each Protestant church Sunday evening for an hour before the evening service. Like the prayer meetings, these discussion hours attract few people, attendance ranging from about fifteen to fifty, almost invariably with girls in the heavy majority. . . . The testimony of those who have followed Middletown's churches over a period of years is unanimous that there is less spontaneous interest in these young people's services today than thirty-five years ago."

Page 126. "Modern men are freer . . . from church ties."

Walter Lippmann: *A Preface to Morals* (New York: The Macmillan Company; 1930), page 59:
"The modern man is an emigrant who lives in a revolutionary society and inherits a protestant tradition. He must be guided by his conscience. But when he searches his conscience, he finds no fixed point outside of it by which he can take his bearings. He does not really believe that there is such a point, because he himself has moved about too fast to fix any point long enough in his mind."

Page 129. "Many are afraid of losing their jobs. . . ."

Robert S. and Helen Merrell Lynd: *Middletown* (New York: Harcourt, Brace & Company; 1929), page 66:

"The chance of promotion as it appears to the working class may be glimpsed from the answers of the wives in 105 of the 124 sample families to the question: 'What seems to be the future in your husband's job?' It was a time of considerable local unemployment. Ten of the 105 husbands were already out of work, and 'future' meant hope for the naked chance to begin getting a living again at anything; for twenty-two other wives future meant nothing beyond the possible date when 'the mister' would be laid off—for two of them this future was no further off than 'next Saturday'; to four others the future meant predominantly a fear of the old-age dead line; to eleven others a 'good' future meant 'He'll probably have steady work'; nineteen others were hopeful in regard to their husbands' work and their chances in it; while the remaining thirty-nine faced the future with no expressed hope of getting ahead. Of these thirty-nine, thirty-two, while not at the moment out of work or driven by an active fear of unemployment, voiced keen discouragement."

Page 130. "A scientific attitude cannot evolve . . ."

See *International Encyclopedia of Unified Science*, Volume I, Number I (Chicago: University of Chicago Press; 1936), especially the articles: Otto Neurath: "Unified Science as Encyclopedic Integration" (pages 1, 23), John Dewey: "Unity of Science as a Social Problem" (pages 29, 38), Charles W. Morris: "Scientific Empiricism" (page 74).

Acknowledgment

I should like to acknowledge the work of my collaborators in the International Foundation for Visual Education, who aided me in expressing my statements by means of the picture-text style: Gerd Arntz, chief of the graphic department, whose genius as we evolved the ISOTYPE method, supported by other designers, created its characteristic graphic style; Miss Marie Reidemeister, who has worked with me from the beginning of our pedagogical and scientific activities, and who, as chief of the transformation department, with her combination of scientific judgment and ability for visualization, did the preparatory work. I should like to thank not only these and other present collaborators of the Institute but also all those who helped to build up our method and to develop our style during the last fifteen years.

I am under special obligation to Waldemar Kaempffert, who not only was for years a friend of our educational and scientific work but also stimulated and helped me to elaborate this book. I also wish to thank my publisher, who was prepared to give me an opportunity to apply the picture-text style to a greater extent than was originally planned, in spite of formidable difficulties.

Date Due

9res.			
	Remington Rand Inc. Cat. no. 1139.		